Her

Resourceful,
a loss for idea
have unexpec

Whether s
at school, ma ... of the free entertainments of a big department store, or trying out free samples from the local icecream shop, she always has the knack of making things happen.

Lively, unsentimental and often funny, these nine short stories of life in every-day city streets and parks will appeal particularly to primary school readers between eight and eleven.

TAKES A HAND

Barbara Paterson

Illustrated by Peter Dennis

A Hippo Book
Scholastic Publications Limited
London

Scholastic Publications Ltd,
161 Fulham Road, London SW3 6SW, England

Scholastic Book Services,
50 West 44th Street, New York 10036, NY, USA

Scholastic Tab Publications Ltd,
123 Newkirk Road, Richmond Hill, Ontario L4C 3G5, Canada

H J Ashton Co Pty Ltd, Box 579,
Gosford, New South Wales, Australia

H J Ashton Co Pty Ltd,
9–11 Fairfax Avenue, Penrose, Auckland, New Zealand

First published by Scholastic Publications Ltd 1980

Typeset by Computacomp (UK) Ltd, Fort William, Scotland
Made and printed in the U.S.A.
Set in Bembo

Contents

HENNY

I

The Day Moggs stayed Awake

'Heavens, look at the time!'

Mrs Cary looked at the kitchen clock and started to push her tea away.

'Go on, Mum, relax!' Michael pushed the cup back towards her. 'We'll get away in time, don't you worry.'

'But you mustn't be late the first day of term.'

'It's much the best day to *be* late,' Henny pointed out, reaching for more toast. 'The teachers are all too busy sorting out the stock and wishing it was still the holidays to notice who's late and who's not.'

'All the same ... Michael, you'll be sure to take Jack right to his room, won't you?'

'Yes, I guarantee to deliver him into his teacher's hands, and to retrieve him again at the end of the afternoon. And make sure you don't budge until I get there. Right?' he said, turning to Jack.

Jack looked up and smiled largely over the top of his cereal bowl. Henny, vividly remembering what that silent smile on her small brother's face had meant over the summer holidays, said sternly:

'Say yes, Jack.'

He gazed at her forgivingly.

'Yes, Henny.'

'I wish you didn't have to go on your own.' Mrs Cary piled her cup and saucer on her plate and started to clear the table.

'Don't be daft, Mum. I'd look a proper charlie if you took *me*, thank you very much!' Michael, starting his second year at the local comprehensive, blenched at the thought.

'You know I didn't mean *you*, Michael! But ...'

'Well, *I've* been going on my own ever since I joined the juniors, and I'm safer on the roads than ever I was!' Henny dropped her knife with an indignant clatter on her plate, and stared accusingly at her mother's back. 'You're forgetting, our class got a certificate in the Panda competition, and *I* was the head of the group that won it.'

'And Jack likes going with me, he's used to it.' Michael's glare challenged his junior to disagree. 'So you see, you've absolutely nothing to worry about. You go off and get on with all that clever shorthand stuff again, and don't bother about anything else. We'll get along fine.'

'Yes, I know you will really. It's just starting again that takes a bit of getting used to. Anyway, I must go—I can't be late *my* first day. *I'd* be pretty certain to get noticed!'

She went next door into the pocket-sized bathroom. There was the sound of teeth being brushed, and she came out moments later with a blue scarf tied over her thick brown hair.

Henny put the milk back in the fridge, stood up and examined her mother critically.

'You look very businesslike in that get-up, with a skirt and shirt, like ladies in offices in the commercials, the ones that say things like "Oh, my girdle's killing me". But I still like you best in jeans and sandals, like you wore when we were away.'

'It's certainly a lot more comfortable, but this is how bosses expect secretaries to look.' She bent down to give Jack and Henny a kiss, and patted Michael on the back. 'See you later, then. Michael, make sure you lock the front door behind you when you leave. Have a good day! Bye!'

Michael took Jack into the bathroom to swab off the milk and cereal, while Henny found and lost and refound her bag of pencils and crayons and rubber, and the frog that went boing, and the sharpener with an elephant from the zoo, and five sticks of rock as presents for Bella and Kim and George and Kevin and Dennis. Finally, all three emerged into the September sunshine.

As they set off down the street, the flowered net curtains of the ground-floor window of the next house in the terrace opened, and old Mr Marston tapped on the window and waved to them.

So the summer holidays were over for another year, he thought to himself. An end to the noise and the scuffling and the big boy's radio and the small boy's car imitations and the other kids pouring in and out of the flat. That flat must be a tight squeeze for the four of them ... Still, if you had to have children next door, you could certainly do worse. It was a pity that the girl hardly ever seemed to wear a pretty dress, it was all trousers these days. And her hair could do with tidying up, all in a mop like that. But she was a cheerful little thing.

Yes.

It would seem very quiet for the next few days.

Henny said good-bye to Michael and Jack at the top of the road, and watched them turn away to the right. They had to walk two streets down to get to Jack's nursery school, and then Michael would catch a bus. Often he walked, but today he was too late.

Henny had to turn to the left, past the shops, and the launderette, and the 'Princess Beatrice', and the Turf Consultants, and the Baptist Chapel, before crossing the main road and walking down Canning Street towards her school.

It was awful getting up early when the holidays were over, she thought; but all the same, she liked this time of day. They were unloading crates outside the dairy. The hairdresser was in the launderette taking clean towels out of the tumble-dryer. A van loaded with bread and buns stood outside the baker's. Henny stopped and sniffed. Even though she'd just finished breakfast the smell made her feel hungry. Across the road the butcher's assistant, in his clean white Monday overall, was giving the shop window its weekly wash. He waved to Henny through the glass as she passed by.

The door of the betting shop stood open. Inside it was empty, the floor clean and swept—not the way it usually looked with men squashed together in a haze of smoke, and the floor littered with bits of paper and cigarette butts.

Outside the 'Princess Beatrice' two women with three small children were waiting to start their morning's cleaning. One of them was Dennis's mother. 'You're goin' to be late, Henny,' she warned, in her soft Irish voice. 'Dennis's been gone these ten minutes.'

Henny ran towards the zebra crossing. She couldn't be very late; the roads were still busy. Groups of older boys were jostling each other and shouting; teenagers were wobbling along in fancy shoes; tiny children even younger than Jack were being whisked along by scurrying mums.

And when she finally turned into Canning Street, there just ahead of her she could see several of her classmates.

Right in front, almost at the school gate, she could see the tall figure of George, already one of the biggest boys in the school, with a woolly hat pulled over his black curly hair, holding the hands of his two younger brothers. That must be Kevin beside him, skinnier than ever, wearing what looked like a new football shirt. On the other side of the road she saw Sharon, easily recognisable with her long black plait and her pink-and-gold-edged trousers.

She couldn't see Kim. Probably she was in the playground already. Her parents opened their shop long before nine o'clock and always packed her off to school in plenty of time. Oh, she couldn't wait to see Kim again!

Henny gave a skip and a jump and started to run. Then she slowed down. Coming out of St Philip's Grove was Stephen Blake, as neat and spotless as ever.

She didn't want to catch him up.

She paused for a moment in front of Neilson's, the little corner shop, and pressed her nose against the window. She couldn't see Moggs anywhere. He must be having his breakfast.

She felt a sudden jolt in her ribs.

'Bella! Ooh, how dare you!'

She poked vigorously back, beaming broadly at the sight of Arabella's red-headed freckled face. 'What—you're *walking* to school?'

Bella shrugged her shoulders.

'Dad got a tax bill again. Aren't you late?'

'I'm starting as I mean to go on. Anyway, if I am so're you.'

'Perhaps, for the first day, we ought to give them a treat ...?'

They started to jog off down the street, linking hands and intoning as they went a chant they had invented at the end of the summer term.

'If no one ever marries me
I think that I'll grow up to be
  A millionaire ...

'If no one ever marries me
I think that I'll grow up to be
  Lazeeeeeeee
  Happeeeeeee ...'

The first day of school passed as the first day of school always did. Henny's class had a new teacher—called Mr Fielding—who seemed all right but was as confused as most new teachers. Bernard and Clive sat as far away as they could and smilingly dropped things and pinched things and tested him and the prospects for the new term. Kim and Rhona and Tracy drew yet more versions of their endless horse sagas. New books were handed out, new timetables explained, new pupils welcomed, and new hopes uttered for the school year.

By the end of the afternoon Henny felt ready to explode. It had been a long hard day.

Freedom lay just outside the gates.

'You coming back with me tonight, Kim? How about you, Bella?'

'I can't, Henny.' Kim pulled on her cardigan. 'Me Mum's goin' to baby-sit tonight for David. She wants me back to lend her a hand with the boxes before she goes.'

'Michael'll want me back too,' said Henny, 'but it'll only be to do the potatoes or something boring like that. You coming, Bella?'

'*Not* to do the potatoes,' she said, spreading out her sun-browned fingers with the topaz ring, and looking at them with great satisfaction. 'I think I'll paint my nails green tonight.'

'You'll look like a witch,' said Henny cheerfully. They dawdled off together picking up the routine of the term before, greeting friendly cats, reading the cards in the tobacconist's window, picking up sweet wrappers hoping to qualify for one of the prizes, until they crossed St Philip's Grove and came to Mr Neilson's shop.

'Tell you what,' said Arabella. 'Let's buy some nuts and raisins.'

'I haven't any money.'

'No, but I have.'

'I thought your Dad was broke again.'

'Not *that* broke.'

Bella hopped up the step and pushed the door.

It stayed shut.

'Funny!' She pushed again.

'The door's stuck again.'

Henny came up behind her and leaned hard against it. It didn't budge.

A large black cat appeared and pawed at the far side of the glass. Henny scratched at the door near the cat's nose. Her finger left a pale smudge. The cat's mouth opened in a silent mew.

Henny grasped the door handle and shook it. The door stayed shut.

The cat abandoned the door and jumped on to the shelf behind the small window, and stalked up and down amid the tins of rhubarb and processed peas.

'What's up with Moggs?' said Henny. 'He's usually sound asleep by now.'

'Mmm, sprawling on the biscuits with a happy smile,' agreed Bella.

The cat disappeared into the back of the shop. Henny leant against the glass door and put her hands against the side of her head to make a screen.

'It's no good. You can't see past the cash desk and those orange plastic bags Mr Neilson's got hanging up.'

'Never mind. You can get peanuts anywhere.'

Arabella jumped back off the step.

'Hang on a minute!' Henny turned away from the door and called after her. 'Do you think something's happened to Mr Neilson?'

'How should I know? Come on. We'll go to one of the shops in the main road.'

'Yes, but listen, Bella, he wouldn't leave Moggs on his own like that.'

Henny stood on the step and looked around. An old woman with a red straw hat came towards them, leaning heavily on a stick.

'Where's Mr Neilson?' Henny was too puzzled to be polite.

'*I* dunno. Ain't opened up today. Please themselves, some of these shopkeepers.'

'But he's always open,' Henny persisted. 'And if he isn't, he puts up a bit of paper saying, "Regret this shop will remain closed owing to holidays" or something like that.'

'It's a proper nuisance 'aving it shut, that I do know. When you can't walk easy, you don't want to go down to the main road. Taken a long weekend, 'e'as. Gone to the seaside, or somewhere like that I expect. Wish I could.'

She plodded dourly on.

'There you are!' Bella had been bouncing up and down during the old lady's slow speech, and was aching to be off. 'Come on, Henny.'

'No, Bella, listen. When I came past this morning, Moggs wasn't there. Right? So he'd gone off to have his breakfast. Right? So Mr Neilson must have been there already. Right? So why hasn't he opened up as usual?'

'Oh, Henny! Moggs wasn't there because he was asleep.'

'Moggs is *never* asleep in the morning. He's always waiting in the window or behind the door until Mr Neilson turns up. And then Mr Neilson gives him his breakfast round the back, and tidies up the shop, and does the till—that kind of thing—and then he unlocks the door and leaves it open. You *know* that. He always does.'

'Well, today he didn't. I dare say he decided to take Monday off, just like she said.'

'He'd never do that. I asked him once if he didn't mind leaving Moggs all alone in the shop, and he said no, Moggs was used to it, and Moggs had to earn his keep, and he did that by catching mice and staying there on Sundays. But he said he never leaves Moggs longer than one day. When Mr Neilson goes away for his holidays he always takes Moggs away and leaves him with a neighbour. He wouldn't leave him here on his own, I'm sure. The point *is*, Bella, that Moggs wasn't there this morning, and now he is.'

'All right. So what? Cats aren't clockwork. Come on, Henny. Let's go.'

'Just supposing ...' said Henny slowly, starting to follow her, 'just supposing Mr Neilson *did* come, as he always does and then something happened to him, so he never gave Moggs his breakfast, and he never came back to unlock the door.'

'What sort of thing?' asked Bella sceptically.

'*I* don't know. Maybe burglars attacked him. Or he broke his leg.'

Henny turned and looked back at the shop, in time to see Moggs leaping back into the window, racing up and down among the tins, still opening his mouth in the mew she couldn't hear.

'Wait until tomorrow, Henny. I bet you'll find the shop open as usual.'

'But supposing something *has* happened, and no one knows anything about it—Mr Neilson lives all on his own. Mrs Neilson died years ago ... *I* know!'

Henny stood back and looked consideringly up at the shop. It was a small brick-built single-storey building squeezed into a long narrow space.

'If I could get up on to the roof—you remember, Bella, there's a skylight at the back of the shop—I could look down, and see if Mr Neilson *is* there. I'd have a good chance of spotting him. It's not a lot higher than the school wall, and I can climb that.'

'But it *is* higher,' Arabella pointed out practically. 'And there aren't any footholds.'

'You could give me a bunk up.'

'I'd get my dress dirty, and you still wouldn't be high enough.'

'You're right. I need someone bigger. Like George. I haven't seen him go by yet, have you?'

She walked round the corner and looked back down the road towards the school.

'Here he comes!'

She jumped up and down and waved furiously.

'All right—where's the fire?' said George, arriving with his two small brothers in tow.

Henny explained, while Bella continued to look resigned.

'Just give me a start, George, and I'll be up on the roof in a flash.'

George looked doubtful.

'I dunno as you should. They'll think you're trying to break in.'

'Not when I explain. Anyway, no one'll see me. It won't take a moment, and once I'm up there I'll keep down flat. Come on, George!'

'Oh do, George! Then maybe she'll be satisfied and I can go off and get my peanuts somewhere else.'

'O.K. Wayne and Henry, you stay right there, or I'll skin the pair of you. If I hadn't've 'ad to go lookin for you all over the playground we'd've been home by now.'

He bent down and Henny climbed on to his back. She was tall but slight for her age, and it was no effort for him to straighten up with her on his shoulders. She reached up and gripped the edge of the flat roof. George grabbed her ankles and pushed, while she pulled hard and scrabbled with her feet.

One last twist and a push, and she was there.

Keeping low, she moved across to where the skylight lay like a patch of cloud fallen on the black roofing. She edged her way forwards until her head and shoulders were over the glass. She lay there for several seconds, peering down. It was very difficult to see in. The glass was dirty and it had wires running through it. There were iron bars across it inside. From the outside, it made a better mirror than a window.

Henny lay there thinking. It would be too humiliating to go back and admit failure. She had an idea. She sat up and took off her denim jacket, lay down again, and spread it over her head, making a small tent, like a black cloth over a photographer's head in a cartoon. She shut her eyes to get them used to the dark. It was a bit like when you went to the pictures. You fell over the seats to start with, and then after you'd trodden on everyone's feet you sat down and found you could see everything perfectly well.

She counted to sixty, then to a hundred, then to a hundred and twenty; and opened her eyes. She found that the glass was no longer the barrier it had been. She could see through the wires and the dirt and the bars into the shop. She could see different-coloured blobs of light and shade where different things were stored on shelves, and the large pale patch which was the deep-freeze. There were square dark shadows which must be boxes waiting to be unpacked, and below her to the right, half-hidden by the top of a shelving unit which cut off her view, a large pale irregular shapeless blotch.

She shut her eyes for a moment. When she opened them again the large pale blotch took shape. It was someone wearing a white overall lying on the floor.

It could only be Mr Neilson.

Henny sat up, pulled on her jacket and ran back to the edge of the roof, scrambled over the edge, hung on for a moment, then let herself go.

'He's there all right! Lying on the floor, right at the back.'

'You're joking!' said Arabella.

'Bet he's been murdered,' said George.

'Don't be daft!' said Henny. 'Who'd want to murder Mr Neilson?'

'You never know,' said George. 'What you goin' to do now?'

'Get the police. And an ambulance.'

'There's a phone box across the road,' said Bella.

'I *know*,' said Henny. 'That's the one Mr Neilson uses for his orders. Come on!'

Henny had never had to make a 999 call before, and she was highly impressed by the results.

First a police car arrived. Then passers-by started to gather. Then one of the policemen climbed on to the roof, and returned to confirm Henny's report. After a short discussion about keys, one of the policemen broke open the lock. Henny and Bella and George had never seen this, except on television, and watched with interest. One policeman went back to the car and put out a call to hurry up the ambulance, while the other stopped anyone else from going into the shop. The ambulance came screeching round the corner, siren sounding, and still more people gathered. The ambulance men went inside, and came out with Mr Neilson lying palely on a stretcher underneath a blanket.

At the sight of his face Henny suddenly forgot to be excited. She went up to the police car and pulled at the jacket of one of the policemen.

'Excuse me,'

'Run along! It's all over now, nothing more to see.'

'Please, I just want to know—he will be all right, won't he?'

Arabella, coming up behind, added 'We're the ones who rang you up.'

'Oh, you are, are you? Well, you shouldn't have been climbing around on roofs. Don't do it again, will you! The bloke—what's his name? Neilson? Well, he was standing on a box to reach something on a shelf, and when he stepped off he somehow got tangled up with the cat. He fell sideways and hit something and found he couldn't move. Looks as if he's broken his hip. He tried shouting, but of course no one could hear him as he was right at the back. He might have been there till who knows when if it hadn't been for you.'

Henny felt a glow spread right through her.

'But he'll be all right?' she persisted.

'Certainly he will. Probably have to stay in the hospital for a while, but he'll be fine, thanks to you.'

'What about Moggs?'

'Moggs?'

'His cat. It was seeing Moggs that got us worried.' Henny and Bella explained, one after the other and both at the same time.

'All right all *right*!' The policeman held up a hand. 'I promise you I'll find someone to take care of Moggs until Mr Neilson comes back. All right?'

'Cross your heart and hope to die?' asked Henny.

'Cross my heart!' said the policeman.

With a wail the ambulance left and the bystanders started to drift away. Moggs crouched balefully in a far corner of the window.

'He'll be all right,' said the policeman. 'Go on home, now.'

Henny and Bella and George and his brothers turned to walk down to the main road.

'Do you think he meant Moggs?' asked Bella. 'Or Mr Neilson?'

'Doesn't matter, really,' said Henny, practically. 'As long as they both are.'

2

Mark and the Missed School Dinners

'Do you know what I think?' said Henny, returning to her seat between Kevin and Kim with a plate of jam roly-poly.

'You didn't get enough custard.'

'You wanted ice cream.'

'No, stupid! I think there's something funny about Mark.'

'Mark? Which Mark?'

'The new Mark. The one who started this term.'

'What sort of funny? He doesn't say much, but he's all right.'

'I quite like him,' said Kim. 'He borrowed me his ruler when I left mine at home.'

'Not that sort of funny ... But haven't you noticed? He hasn't stayed for dinner all this week. And I don't think he had dinners last week either.'

'So what? Philip goes back to his Mum's caff, and George goes out and gets chips ...'

'And Tracy goes home so's 'er Mum can do up 'er 'air in those poncy ringlets ...'

'Yes, I *know*, but he always had dinners when he first came ...'

'I dare say he got fed up with chewed string ...'

'And frogspawn ...'

'And boiled baby mice ...'

'No, *listen*. You know Rhona always brings sandwiches? Well, her Mum always makes her heaps—no wonder she's so fat, and sometimes even *she* can't finish them. Yesterday when we went back into the classroom I saw Mark look round quickly to make sure no one was watching, and pull out the bag Rhona'd chucked in the bin. When he went over in the corner to get on with his project and he thought no one'd notice, I saw him polish off what she'd left. All I can say is he didn't look like someone who'd just had dinner.'

'You didn't say anything about it yesterday.'

'I forgot,' said Henny frankly. 'I only remembered about it just now, when I went for my pudding, and I looked around and he's not here again.'

Kevin picked up his plate and pushed back his chair.

'If you want to know where he goes at dinner-time, why don't you ask him?'

'You're right,' said Henny, scraping up the last crumbs. 'I'll get my seconds first, and then I'll go and look for him.'

Mark wasn't in the playground when she went out. He wasn't playing football. Or British bulldog. Or flicking cards. It wasn't until a minute before the bell went that she saw him coming through the school gate at the far side.

There were dirty smears on his face and his eyes looked pink. She watched him stop by the water fountain and hold his head over the spray, then wipe his shirt sleeve over his dripping face.

'Hello!' she said, speeding to catch up with him. 'You're a bit damp. You missed a good dinner today. Roly-poly and custard. Almost my best pudding.'

She glanced sideways at him.

He looked down at his feet and said nothing.

'Still, I suppose your Mum's dinners're even better.'

He muttered something Henny couldn't hear.

'What?'

'I said, I haven't got a Mum.' He glared at her.

'Sorry,' she said, catching up with him again in the corridor. Awkwardly, they walked side by side towards the classroom. 'I never meant...' She paused, uncertainly.

He said nothing.

Round them the noise began to die away as they reached the classroom door.

Mr Fielding was hanging something on the blackboard.

'Come along now, settle down, less noise at the back there. Henny, shut the door. Mark, you're going to be last again ...'

He unrolled the map with a final clatter, and Mark and Henny separated to go to their own places.

She didn't get another chance to speak to him until the end of the afternoon. Then, instead of leaving the school by the blue gate as usual, she followed him out through the black one.

'Hi!' she said, catching him up. 'I've got to go back this way today.'

'Why?' he asked suspiciously.

Henny thought fast.

'Because I promised my little brother I'd go in to that Indian shop that sells toys and see if they'd got one of those new whirligigs there. Not that he can buy it, he's too small to get pocket money, but I said I'd look ... Have you got any brothers and sisters?'

He shook his head.

'No,' he said shortly. 'There's just me.'

They walked along side by side. He said nothing further to her, but kept tweaking leaves from the privet hedges alongside, screwing them into little green heaps and dropping them on the pavement. Henny glanced at him, uncertain what to say next. She wished she hadn't noticed anything odd about Mark, wished she'd gone out of the blue gate. Still ...

'It's funny really,' she said suddenly. 'You haven't got a Mum. Well, I haven't got a Dad. Nor's Rhona. And Martin lives with his Nan.'

'What happened to your Dad?'

'He went away. Ages ago. When Jack—that's my little brother—was a baby. He kept crying a lot. Jack, I mean, not my Dad. He'd got something wrong with one of his ears, only no one knew. Then one day, after my Dad'd gone, he screamed and screamed and something went pop in his ear and stuff came out and after that he was better. Now he's ever so good and hardly ever cries. My Mum says he got over all his temper in the first six months.'

'I dare say your Dad got tired of hearing him.'

'Maybe. Mind you, he was always away a lot anyhow. Travelling around. Something to do with buying and selling. He sends us postcards sometimes. From America mostly. That's where he lives now, since he got married again.'

There was silence again.

'My Mum died,' said Mark suddenly. 'She got killed in an accident last year. A friend was taking her shopping in her car, a lorry hit the car at a crossroads, and my Mum got killed.'

'That's awful,' said Henny.

Mark nodded, silently.

'Bye, Henny! See you tomorrow!' Dennis shouted as he ran past and crossed the street.

'And don't forget to bring your football!' shouted Kevin, following him. 'Cheers, Mark!'

Mark didn't answer. He trudged along, head down.

'What do they call you Henny for?' he said, obviously changing the subject.

'My real name's Penelope. Something to do with my father being away a lot—I'm not sure why. I used to be called Penny. And then when I went to my first school, the teacher read out the story about Henny Penny. You know, Chicken Licken and the sky a-falling? And the others started calling me Henny Penny, as a joke, and the Henny bit stuck. Only Granny Cary calls me Penelope now.'

They went on walking.

This was getting them nowhere, thought Henny.

Abruptly, she stopped in her tracks.

'Mark! Why don't you have school dinners any more?'

For a minute Henny thought he hadn't heard. He walked on in front of her, kicking an empty matchbox along the street.

'Why not, Mark? I mean, your Dad ...'

'Because I *can't*, that's why not!' Mark shouted, and kicked the matchbox savagely off the pavement.

'What do you mean, you can't?'

Mark stopped. He looked around him; then he turned to face Henny.

'I can't because I can't pay for it. I can't pay because my money gets nicked every morning.'

Henny looked round too.

'Who by?'

Mark turned away. Henny barely heard as he muttered down into his thick sweater: 'He said he'd put his mates on to me if I breathed a word.'

'But he's not here now, is he?'

Mark shook his head.

'So he won't know, will he? *You're* not going to tell him, and *I* won't. Bet I can guess who it is, anyway. It's someone in school?'

Mark nodded.

'In our class?'

Another nod.

'Bigger than you?'

'Well, of *course* he's bigger than me!' said Mark, exasperated. 'I'm not stupid. I wouldn't let him take it if I could stop him. The first time it happened, he took me by surprise. He came across and said had I remembered my dinner money, and when I felt my pocket and said yes, he grabbed hold of me and took it out. The next day, he was waiting round the corner, and he jumped me. And it's been like that ever since. I've tried coming different times, and different ways, but it's no good, sooner or later I've got to come down Sinclair Road, and if he hasn't got me before he always grabs me there.'

'I can be pretty sure who it is then. Stephen Blake.'

Mark nodded reluctantly.

'How did you know?'

'It's the sort of thing he does. And he's the one who lives round here.'

'He doesn't look it though, does he? When I first came, I thought he was all right. I mean, he smiles a lot, and he doesn't go round bashing like Bernard in the playground, knocking over Sixes—at least not very often.'

'Only when he thinks no one can see him,' agreed Henny. 'Not teachers, that is. That's him all over. I don't think he's ever been in trouble. Not real trouble. He's careful. He sets Clive on, though, haven't you noticed? He lets Clive catch it instead.'

'I suppose you think I'm pretty feeble, letting him get away with it.' Mark turned to face Henny, his eyes big with misery. 'Only I don't see what I can *do*. He's *miles* bigger and heavier than me, *and* he can run faster. I tried to race him, but he caught up easily. He said if I told Sir he'd say it was all lies, that he'd seen me buying packets of crisps, and then he'd get his mates on to me the moment school was over. And I haven't any friends here yet. Not that you could really call *friends*. Hardly anyone lives along this way anyhow.'

He started walking on again. The sky was grey and the air smelt of soot and petrol.

'Wish we'd never come here. I was all right where we were.'

Henny padded along beside him.

'What about telling your Dad?'

'I can't do that. He only just started this new job, and he gets back dead tired. I *can't* tell him now.'

Henny understood.

'We've just got to think of something ourselves ... Is he always on his own? He doesn't have Bernard or Clive with him? Then I'm not sure he *would* get his mates on to you. He'll want to keep the money himself.'

'It's not exactly a chance I want to take,' Mark pointed out grimly. 'Every one of them's bigger than I am.'

'Course not, but listen! Steve wouldn't dish out a penny if he didn't have to. He's mean. And though Bernard and Clive are quite capable of bashing people up for no reason at all, they'd be a bit suspicious if Steve just asked them to out of the blue. He's already got them into pretty bad trouble a couple of times this term. I don't think they're wanting any more.'

Mark stopped, and sat down on a low wall between the bits of sawn-off metal where long ago the railings had been taken away.

'Let's hope you're right. But I still don't see what I can do.'

'You can't just give in!' said Henny. 'He won't stop unless he's made to. I can see why you don't want to bother your Dad, but what about telling Sir?'

'Even if I wanted to risk getting beaten up, and I don't, what Steve said is right. If he swears everything I say's lies, who's Sir going to believe? He's new same as I am. As far as he knows, I might be the kind of kid who goes round doing whatever Steve says I've been up to. And teachers believe Steve, you know. I've watched them.'

'They do *seem* to,' said Henny cautiously. 'He's clever. He never puts a foot wrong. I'm not sure they all do, though. I'm pretty certain Miss last year didn't. If she hadn't gone off to have her baby you could have told her.'

'Well, she did, and I don't want to tell Sir, and that's flat. I don't think it'd do any good anyway. Even if you're right about Clive and Bernard, Steve's quite big enough to beat me up on his own.'

'I'll try and think of something,' promised Henny. 'I've got to go now, Mark, or Michael'll be mad at me. Where d'you live, exactly? If I get any bright ideas I'll come round and tell you.'

'5 Stanbeck Villas. It's a flat in a house down at the end of Stanbeck Road. There's a junk-shop opposite.'

'I know where you mean. If I think of anything, I'll come round later and tell you, as long as it's not too late.'

Mark stood up, and dusted down his trousers.

'I don't see what you *can* think of,' he said gloomily. 'But thanks anyway, Henny. I feel better now someone knows.'

Henny was still brooding over Mark's problem when she reached home and rang the bell.

'You're late!' said Michael. He looked hot and cross. 'Where've you been?' He didn't wait for an answer, but turned and hurried back along the narrow hallway to the kitchen, from which a pale blue-grey cloud was drifting.

'Ooh, pancakes!' sniffed Henny hungrily. 'That's a great idea.'

'Yeah, well, I burnt the first one 'cause Jack went and threw his milk all over everywhere.'

'Didn't throw,' protested Jack. 'It was a haccident!' He was sitting at the table gazing sorrowfully at a half-wiped up streaky patch before him. 'Only a haccident!' Tears gathered in his eyes and threatened to spill over.

'All right, all right! Henny, make yourself useful—mop up the floor before we all start skating on it.'

Henny dumped her school-bag on the table well out of Jack's way, and went to fetch the floor-cloth.

'Take one of the bowls from the cupboard under the sink,' said Michael, turning back to the stove, 'or you'll be dripping milk all over the place.'

Henny mopped and squeezed, and mopped and squeezed, until the pool at Jack's feet had dwindled to a puddle and then to a gleaming circle.

'I expect you could use milk to polish the floor,' she said, emptying the bowl in the sink and bending down to put it away. 'It always seems to leave it shiny.'

'It'd be a pretty expensive sort of polish.' Michael tipped a pancake on a plate and spread it with jam and rolled it up. 'Here, Jack, and don't you go hurling this around.'

Henny, trying to push the bowl to the back of the cupboard, felt it stick half-way.

'Bother,' she said crossly, pushing hard. 'What's the matter with the stupid thing? If I got it out it must go back again.'

'Don't just keep shoving then. Have a look and see what's stopping it.'

Groaning, Henny squatted down and peered into the dark inside. Right at the back was a cardboard box. She reached in and pulled it out.

'That's it! I must have shifted the box when I took the bowl out. I wonder what Mum put it here for?' She opened up the top and looked inside. 'Mousetraps! Ugh!'

'They've been there for donkey's years,' said Michael. 'Come on, leave them alone, your first pancake's almost ready. Don't you remember how we had mice when we first moved in? They ran all over the kichen and munched holes in the packets and chewed the edge of the frying pan.'

'Yuk!' said Henny, but half-heartedly. Her mind was not on mice. A brilliant idea had come into her head, and while she ate pancakes and drank tea she turned it over in her mind.

'You're quiet!' said Michael suspiciously. 'What's up?'

'Nothing's up,' said Henny blandly. Michael did not always appreciate the beauty of her ideas.

She helped Michael to clear up and washed Jack's sticky paws, and waited impatiently for her mother to come home. While Michael and Jack were down in the front room watching the television she opened the cupboard under the sink again and slipped one of the mousetraps into her pocket.

As soon as she heard her mother's key in the latch Henny darted into the hall.

'It's all right if I go out for a bit, isn't it, Mum?'

'You might wait until I've got through the door! Why do you want to go out now anyway?' She untied her scarf and ran her fingers through her hair, yawning. 'I thought I was never going to get back tonight. I started to walk, there were so many people waiting for the bus. Besides, what about some supper?'

'I only want to go and see Mark for a bit, Mum, I said I might call in. I won't be long, and he's not far away, only 5 Stanbeck Villas. And I don't need any supper, Michael made us heaps of pancakes because he came back starving. Go on, Mum! I'll be back in half an hour.'

'All right. Mind, Henny, that doesn't mean staying till all hours! I want you back by the time I've got Jack to bed.'

'Course, Mum! Thanks, Mum!'

Henny reached up and kissed her mother, picked up her anorak, and disappeared through the front door before there could be any change of mind.

Stanbeck Villas was a tall house in dark red brick and tall windows and a tall thin black door. When Henny pressed the bell by the piece of paper marked Flat 5, she could hear nothing at all except, from somewhere inside, the sound of someone's television.

I hope there's someone there after all that effort, she thought, and pressed again. There were footsteps along a bare floor inside, and the door opened. Mark peered out at Henny. In the frame of the tall thin door he looked small and slight.

'Henny!'

'Yes, got it in one,' said Henny impatiently. 'Well, aren't you going to ask me in?' As Mark silently pulled open the door and stood back, she walked past saying, 'I've had this terrific idea. At least, I *think* it'll work.'

Apprehension flashed over Mark's face. He pressed the light switch at the bottom of the stairs.

'We'll go in the kitchen. Dad's watching the telly in the front room. Come on, Henny. You've got to run, or you get stuck between landings when the lights go off.'

Henny leaped after him up the steps, and with a pause for another push at the light switch on the first floor they almost made it to the top before the lights vanished.

'I bet I could work out a way to make them stay on,' said Henny, following Mark through the open door at the top, 'but it's more fun really the way they are now.'

'Yes, it is,' said Mark firmly. 'Dad, it's a friend from school,' he called through the half-open door to the right. 'We're going in the kitchen, O.K.?'

There were muffled noises of agreement against a background of gunshots, and Mark steered Henny to the glass door at the back of the hall. Inside, the kitchen was immaculate: bright yellow Formica gleamed, all the cupboard doors were shut and nothing sat around on window-sills or tops, in contrast to Henny's flat where plants in pots jostled for space with bits of Jack's jigsaw puzzles and toy cars and pieces of Michael's half-completed experiments.

'You want a biscuit, or orange squash or something?'

'Business before pleasure,' said Henny. 'Besides, I promised Mum I wouldn't be late.' The metal chair squeaked as she pulled it away from the breakfast bar and sat down. 'Look, here it is.' She wriggled the mousetrap free from her pocket and placed it down on the gleaming yellow surface.

Mark gazed down at it.

'What's that for? *We've* got no mice. Our kitchen's clean. Dad's ever so particular.'

'Don't be daft, Mark! It's for Steve, not your Dad. Look, didn't you say that the first day he actually took the money out of your pocket? Well, tomorrow you tell him you haven't got any. He won't believe you. He'll go through your pockets. And then—wham!'

'Wham?' Mark looked at her as though she'd gone mad.

'Wham! The mousetrap will slam shut. Right on his hand. See?' Henny gazed at him triumphantly.

Mark stared at her.

'He'll murder me,' he said simply.

'It's a risk,' said Henny judiciously. 'But I don't think so. Listen! I'll be there, in a gateway or something. I'll get Kevin to come too, if I can. You do your best to keep out of his way the moment it's happened, and I'll tell him if he doesn't stop this racket we'll all tell Sir. And if we do tell Sir he'll believe us, because however else could he get his hand caught in a mousetrap?'

'It'll never work.'

'Yes, it *will*. It's psy-psychology. You don't know Steve like I do. He won't risk having anything pinned on him for certain. He never has. He won't love us for it, but he'll go along with it. You'll see.'

'It won't go off. Or it'll go off at the wrong time. Or it'll go off and it won't get him.'

'Of *course* it'll go off! Look.' Henny picked up the mousetrap. Delicately, she pulled back the spring and hooked the bar over the top. '"The Little Pincher!" What a great name. Let's hope it little pinches him. Now, give me a teaspoon.'

Mark opened a drawer and handed over a teaspoon without a word.

There was a moment's silence as Henny crept the teaspoon nearer and nearer to the trap.

She touched the triggered platform.

Zap!

The metal gate slammed shut. The teaspoon shot out of Henny's hand and clattered to the table.

'Wow!' said Mark.

'You see?' said Henny with satisfaction. 'It works all right. And as long as you set it properly, and put it in your pocket carefully, and *don't* set it off yourself, it can't fail.'

Mark looked at the trap with distrust.

'Supposing it broke his fingers?'

'Serve him right if it did,' said Henny uncharitably. 'But I don't expect it will. Got a pencil handy?'

Mark got up and fetched a memory board leaning on the window-sill. Henny set up the trap again and picked up the red pencil tied to the board. Gently she pushed the pencil forward.

The trap slammed shut with the same vigour as before, and this time held the pencil tightly in its jaws. Henny pulled it free.

'There you are. Nothing broken. But you can see where the paint's cracked here—and here. It's bound to leave a mark, and that's what matters. Isn't it?'

'I don't know.' Mark picked up the memory board and propped it back against the window. 'I don't think we ought to.'

'For heaven's sake, Mark! The trap'll be in your pocket, right? And Steve's got no business messing around in your pockets, right? So if his fingers get caught in The Little Pincher, it's his fault, right? And what else are you going to do? Are you just going to let Steve go on and on helping himself? The longer he keeps going the harder it'll be to stop him. You can't go on waiting for Rhona's cast-off sandwiches for the rest of term.'

Perhaps it was discovering that Henny knew about the sandwiches, or the sudden silence in the background as the television was turned off, but Mark stopped arguing, picked up the mousetrap, and stuffed it hurriedly in his pocket. They heard the front room door shut, and hastily arranged a meeting-place and time: and when Mr Sinclair opened the kitchen door Henny was already standing up and on her way out.

'Going already?' he said. 'Thanks for coming. Mark misses his old friends, I know. Mind you call again, now.'

'See you tomorrow then, Henny?' Mark gazed at her anxiously. 'You're sure you'll be there?'

Henny nodded.

'Of *course* she'll be there.' Mr Sinclair put his arm round Mark's shoulders. 'And so will you. You'll be at school as bright and early as ever if I've anything to do with it. Goodnight then! Going to see your young lady out?'

Mark was silent on the way downstairs.

As he opened the big front door, Henny turned to him.

'You're not going to back out, are you, Mark? I'm not getting up early for nothing.'

'I said I'd do it, Henny, and I will. See you tomorrow.'

'Good luck, Mark!'

He nodded.

'I'll need it.'

Henny went home via Kevin's. She found him sitting on the step outside his house, watching his older brother work on his motorbike. Henny sat down beside him.

'Brr!' she said. 'It's getting really chilly in the evenings now.'

'What you doing here then? Just out for a walk?'

Henny shook her head, and in between bursts of engine noise filled Kevin in on Mark's story.

'Thing is, Kevin, I wish you'd come too. It's not a lot out of your way, and if there were three of us there ... *Please* come, Kev. It'd make such a difference.

Kevin looked reluctant.

'Why don't you ask George? He's bigger than me, and he never minds a bundle.'

'There's no point, Kev. He's got to take his brothers to school. Anyway, you know Steve never *fights*—he gets Bernard to do it for him.'

'Steve doesn't have to fight,' pointed out Kevin. 'Not when he's that big.'

'All the same, he can't bash three of us at once. And anyway, once he's got his hand stuck in the mousetrap, he'll have other things on his mind. I wouldn't want to be there myself otherwise. Do come, Kev.'

It took a little while longer, and a blend of persuasion, flattery, and bribery, but eventually Kevin agreed. Henny went home feeling she had done all she could for the present.

Next day Mrs Cary found Henny already up and finishing her breakfast when she entered the kitchen. 'Miracles will never cease,' she remarked, but asked no questions, and Henny managed to slip out of the house with plenty of time in hand.

It was a damp, misty autumn day. Yesterday's plan had lost a lot of its appeal. Henny found she was no longer as sure as she had been that it couldn't possibly fail. And part of her hoped that Mark might have given up the idea altogether.

Suppose the mousetrap didn't work? Suppose Steve

suspected something? Suppose Kevin had changed his mind?

But Kevin was there waiting at the corner by the second-hand car lot.

'I thought you mightn't come after all!' they both exclaimed at the same moment, and grinned at each other with relief.

'Come on, let's hurry. We've got to get to the big house before Mark does.'

'The one that's the nurses' home?'

'Yes. We'll stand behind the pillars there and we can see through the hedge. Somebody cut it last week, and it's bare at the bottom.'

Side by side they took up their positions, peering through the twigs.

'Are you sure Steve'll jump Mark here?'

'He has the last couple of days, Mark says. Nobody can spot him here. The hedge is too high for anyone from the house to see, even if anyone was looking. And across the road there's just the factory wall.'

'Why does Mark keep coming this way for then?'

'He hasn't got much choice, has he? He did try getting up earlier and going round the factory, but Steve—hey, look! Here comes Steve now, across the road over there by the factory gate. He's slowing down ... he's stopping.'

They watched him turn just inside the opening, and take up his stand under a large black board with VACANCIES printed along the top. He leaned there, waiting. A car passed. Then a bicycle. With a clickety-clack of heels two women passed chattering on their way to work.

'I hope Mark's coming.' Although Steve couldn't possibly hear Kevin found himself half-whispering.

'He's bound to be here soon. His Dad sees him off to school before he goes to work.'

'You can't see much from here. I'll take a quick look

round the pillar and see if he's down the road.'

'No, Kevin!' Henny grabbed hold of him. 'You'll ruin everything if Steve catches sight of us. I told Mark to keep this side of the road. Ssh! I can hear someone coming.'

Steve straightened up. They glimpsed a shape beginning to pass the hedge and as it drew level with them they saw it was Mark.

Steve was crossing the road.

'Wotcher, mate! Dead on time, that's what we like. Come on then, don't hang about. Hand it over. Don't go wastin' me time.'

'I ain't got none today. My Dad didn't have no change. Said to tell Sir he'd pay double tomorrow.'

'Don't give me that. I don't believe you. Still, it's easy enough to find out, innit? No problem. Come 'ere, you.'

Steve grabbed hold of Mark with one hand, swung him round, and thrust the other into his right hand trouser pocket.

The next instant there was a piercing yell.

Steve leapt in the air and let go of Mark, who shot into the gateway beside Kevin and Henny.

For a moment Steve stood there hopping from foot to foot, a stunned expression on his face and the mousetrap firmly fixed to his flapping right hand.

'Geroff! Geroff!' he screeched, presumably under the impression that he had been attacked by some strange animal. Then, as realisation dawned, he stood staring at his hand. With his left hand he tried to pull up the spring, but all he managed to do was to open and immediately shut the trap again. Shrieking with pain and shock, he tried again. Watching in delight, Henny and Kevin and Mark saw him free his right hand only to have the trap shut instantly on his left.

Henny nudged the other two.

'Now's the time.'

They stepped out.

'You! I might've guessed!' Steve lunged towards them. Henny sprang one way, Kevin another.

'Now just you listen, Steve! Any more trouble with Mark and I'll tell Sir. And Kevin'll back me up.' Kevin nodded, but with a wary eye and keeping well out of reach, 'And I'll tell him exactly what happened today and where you got the sore hand you're going to be complaining about at school today. *And*,' she took a stab in the dark '*and* I'll tell Brian and Clive all about your little racket and how you didn't share any of the money with them. See?'

Steve saw.

As Kevin and Henny and Mark headed down the road towards school they turned back for one last glimpse. Steve was poking at his hand with what appeared to be some kind of stick. Two nurses who had walked out of the nurses' home stood for a moment looking at him with curiosity, then shaking their heads at each other they pulled their cloaks over their shoulders and came laughing towards them.

'Playing with mousetraps!' said one of them as they passed. 'Some youngsters haven't the sense they were born with!'

It was cheese pie and cabbage and syrup stodge and custard for dinner. Only Henny's third favourite. But Mark ate every scrap and said it was great.

3

Daisy Ices dish it Out

'I'm going to have a really good breakfast today,' announced Henny, arriving at the kitchen door. 'I'm going to have cereal *and* egg *and* toast *and* golden syrup *and* cocoa.'

'Henny, don't be daft, you're late already!'

'I *told* you, Mum. I brought you the letter last week. They've got someone in mending the boilers, and there *isn't* any school today.'

'Heavens, yes, I'd forgotten. And you're going over to Arabella's. That's still all right then? Mrs Roach hasn't changed her mind? You're sure you won't be in the way?'

'No, of course not, Mum. She's expecting me some time after breakfast. Now don't worry—I'll wash up the things and put out the milk bottles and I'll lock up properly *and* I won't lose the keys. Look—Mike's given me them already and I've got them round my neck.'

'I suppose that's all right,' said Mrs Cary doubtfully. She put down a half-eaten piece of toast. 'I hate leaving you here on your own, but I daren't be late. We're so busy at the moment, I don't know whether I'm coming or going. Well, at least tomorrow's Saturday! Henny, you won't hang around on your own though, will you? You'll go straight to Arabella's?'

'Yes, of course I will. What's wrong with that toast? And why are you rushing off without your egg? You need a proper breakfast. You're always telling us that.'

'Don't boss me, Henny.' Mrs Cary reached across

and gently tugged one of Henny's wiry curls. 'I'll eat it tomorrow chopped up on my toast. Thanks for doing it, Mike, but I've got to fly.' She lifted Jack off his chair, wiped his mouth and gave him a kiss. 'Have a great day at school, and paint me heaps of pictures. See you later.'

After Michael and Jack left the flat suddenly seemed very empty. The dishes clattered as she put them in the sink. The milk bottles rattled against each other as she rinsed them. As she set them down outside the front door the street felt odd. The day seemed out of balance. Not quite a schoolday. Not quite Saturday.

She shut the front door and the flat felt large around her. In the front room her mother had already taken the bedthings off the couch and put them away in the trunk under the window. Henny tipped up the sofa back and arms, and hey presto, it was a living-room and no longer a bedroom.

Picking up a mug from the table near the fireplace, and carrying it back into the kitchen, Henny paused to glance into her room. Even that was somehow less welcoming than usual. Michael's room too felt lonely. His transistor, on the shelf by his bed, seemed to be waiting for him to return and switch it on. There was no sound from Mr Marston's flat in the house next door, and none from the one upstairs—the Nicholsons both had a long journey to work and left early every day.

Henny decided that on the whole you could have too much peace and quiet, and that Arabella was welcome to the big bedroom with the green carpet and the fitted cupboards she had all to herself.

She raced through the dishes, and locked the front door behind her with a sense of release.

If she was lucky, she might be allowed to help in one of the Roaches' two shops. The left-hand one, *Douglas Roach, ANTIQUES*, sold more interesting things.

Henny always stopped and peered through the window to see what was new, and enjoyed it when she was allowed to wander round inside. She liked searching through boxes of old postcards, or opening the brass-handled chests of drawers, or turning the pages of the old books on the shelves behind the door.

On the other hand, Mr Roach was a nervous man. He twitched when she moved too near the delicately painted plates displayed on the dresser at the back, and shuddered when she approached the decanters in the window to see the rainbows trapped in their stoppers. Sometimes his nerves would snap, and he would banish Arabella and Henny next door.

There, in the right-hand one, *Jessica Roach, DECOR*, there was never anything marvellously unexpected, such as an old kaleidoscope or Victorian bricks, but there was nothing to break either, and Jessica (she refused to be called Mrs Roach) never turned a hair when Bella and Henny sorted through piles of lace-trimmed pillowcases and embroidered tablecloths, or reorganised the displays of tapestry firescreens and patchwork cushions. She was as placid as her husband was jittery.

On balance, Henny decided, it might be safer to start in DECOR and wait for Mr Roach's breakfast to settle before venturing into ANTIQUES.

But she could see from across the road that, although it was long past opening time, there was no sign of Mrs Roach—Jessica, sorry—sitting in her usual place beneath the gold letters on the window.

She crossed over and found an elegantly-written notice on the door. It said, 'Jessica Roach will be back shortly. Meanwhile, please apply to ANTIQUES.'

Mr Roach looked up as the doorbell rang. He was sitting behind his desk writing in a large ledger. There was no one else in the shop.

'Ah, yes! Arabella's young friend. Now, what was it

I was to tell you?' He looked back anxiously to his ledger, as though he expected to find a message written there. 'Yes, yes, that's right. You're not at school today, Arabella tells me. Always having holidays, you young people. Yes ... no ... my wife says could you run along to the house. Something's cropped up next door, and I fancy she thought you and Arabella might be able to help her out. Something to do with ribbon, braid; something like that. So you cut off there straight away, there's a good girl, yes?'

Henny nodded.

'Goodbye. Perhaps I'll see you later,' she added politely. Mr Roach winced as he picked up his pen, and failed to express pleasure at the prospect.

The Roaches lived in a tall thin house painted navy blue with white windowframes and a yellow door. Henny pressed the bell, and waited.

No one came. Henny sighed. They still hadn't fixed it; the bell had been broken for weeks. There was a fine brass knocker with a ship's anchor, but it was too high for Henny to reach and she had, as usual, to resort to rattling the letter box. When there was still no sound of footsteps, she bent down and shouted:

'Hey, Bella, Bella, it's me! It's Henny!'

From the far end of the house she could hear the kitchen door slam, and a moment later Mrs Roach was smiling down on her.

'Oh dear,' she said as always. 'The bell isn't working, is it? I really must get it fixed. It's too annoying, the way little things always need seeing to. Arabella, Henny's here.'

With a clash and a clatter Bella came bounding down the stairs.

'Arabella, darling!' protested her mother mildly. 'You'll trip over your dress if you rush everwhere like that.'

'Well, I haven't yet,' said Arabella cheerfully. She and her mother were wearing matching clothes: long navy dresses with tiny yellow flowers half covered by white smocks—to go with their house, thought Henny. 'Come on, Jess—tell Henny what we've planned for this morning.'

Henny followed them into the large room which ran from front to back of the house.

'Goodness!' she said, stopping on the threshold. 'I haven't seen those before!'

Facing her, against the opposite wall, was a large set of shelves loaded with glass cases; and in the glass cases, perched on dried twigs or standing on mounds of pebbles, were what seemed like hundreds of stuffed birds.

'No, dear. Douglas only bought them last week. Do you like them?'

'Not much,' said Henny frankly. 'And aren't there rather a lot of them?'

'Actually,' said Bella, 'they're *maturing*. Dad thinks they're going to be worth a lot more money soon, so he's keeping them here until they are.'

She led the way to the huge leather sofa under the window. As Henny followed, she watched the birds bob silently up and down.

'They look alive.'

'It's only the loose floorboards, sweetie. That builder never fixed them properly, and ever since the carpet's been down it's been too late. One of these days we'll have to get him back again ... Still, never mind that now! Here's what I'd like you to do. It's quite simple.'

The three of them plumped down into the sofa, and Mrs Roach pulled a large wooden box with brass handles and brass metal strips towards her. She pulled the handles apart, and the box sprang open into sets of drawers, full of buttons, cottons, hooks, silks, wools, ribbons and laces. She took out a small packet wrapped in tissue paper, and opened it to show them a short length of twisted creamy silk braid.

'One of my customers rang up this morning to say she's made a mistake, and she wants two extra cushion covers by the weekend. I've enough material, and I can just about do it in the time, but this is all the braid I've got left. I've rung up Peterson's, and they've still got some, so could you go and pick it up? Do you think your mother would mind, Henny? I wouldn't want Arabella to go on her own, but if the two of you are together ...'

'We'll be all right, Mrs Ro—Jessica. I know which bus to get.'

'And *I* know where to get off. I went with you last time, Jess, don't you remember?'

'So you did. I'll go and get the money then. And mind you go straight there. You'll be back in plenty of time for lunch.'

'Ooh, good!' said Arabella, fetching her cloak as her mother vanished upstairs. It's great going out on our own. We'll be able to go up and down all the escalators and have a really good look at the toy department.'

'Makes a great change from school,' agreed Henny. The bus came along before they'd had time to have more than one minor disagreement, so they got on and went upstairs in a state of high good humour.

There was always something new to see to pass the journey. Workmen on scaffolding; two police cars; a lorry with a flat tyre; a totter holding up a long queue of traffic behind him; a fire engine. They sat in the sun that streamed through the front windows, and enjoyed the unaccustomed holiday.

'They needn't really have shut the school today,' pointed out Henny as they got off. 'We could almost have done without heating. It hardly feels wintry at all.'

'You're right—I'm boiling! Cor, look at him! I wouldn't mind some of that.'

Arabella gazed enviously at the old man standing by the main doors of Peterson's. He had taken off his sandwich boards (the one facing them read: 'THERE'S MORE TO LIFE THAN YOU THINK') and was licking a large green ice-cream cone; in his other hand he held an orange one which was beginning to drip on to the pavement.

'It's no good wishing,' said Henny. 'I'm broke. I haven't a penny till I get my pocket money tomorrow.'

The old man saw them looking. He waved his orange ice cream at them. Drops flicked over Bella's cloak.

'There's plenty more where this came from, duck. You take a look round the corner. Fourteen different flavours they've got there.'

'Sounds great!' Henny licked her lips.

'Let's go and get the braid first. If there's change left over, Mum said it'd be OK to spend it.'

They hurried inside.

The braids and ribbons counter was full of two very large ladies arguing over cards of shiny black fringing.

They seemed to be fully prepared to camp there for the rest of the day. The heating was going full blast. There was only one assistant behind the counter, and Henny and Bella were hot, sticky and irritable before their turn finally came.

The assistant took the piece of braid that Arabella handed her, and checked it through her gold-rimmed glasses.

'Yes, I remember. I spoke to your mother earlier this morning, didn't I? I thought this was the one she meant. I put the card aside.'

She unpinned the end of the braid and began to measure it out.

Suddenly she stopped and clicked her tongue.

'Oh no! There's a flaw here towards the end.' She pointed to a small patch where strands of the braid were loose and looped instead of neatly interwoven. 'I can't sell you that, and without it I'm short. What do you think? I've got another one here that's similar but narrower.'

'No, that's no good,' said Bella firmly. 'She's already made the other covers, and the ones she's making now have got to match.'

'We might have some more in the stockroom. I'll ring up and check.'

She came back smiling.

'Yes, that's all right. Shall I send it to you?'

'No, thank you. Mum's got to have it today.'

'Then I'm afraid you'll have to wait for a bit. I can't go until my assistant gets back. She shouldn't be long. All right?'

Her eyes were already flickering past them to a short woman standing behind them with a flustered expression and a piece of yellow material in her hands.

Henny and Bella nodded reluctantly and walked away from the counter.

'Bother!' said Bella. 'I really could do with some of that ice cream, but it's no good going till we've got the change.'

'You're sure your Mum won't mind?'

'No, of course not. She said to get a packet of peanuts if we wanted, and ice cream's just as good. Better, on a day like this.'

'Well, let's hope we don't have to wait too long. Come on, let's go and have a look at something.'

They went and sprayed each other with free samples of *Ecstasy* and *Passionflower*. They watched a lady being transformed by make-up from someone disagreeable and dull into someone disagreeable and brightly-coloured. They sampled pieces of cucumber and carrot from a man demonstrating an electric slicer. They took a lift to the top, and escalators all the way down, then escalators to the top and a lift back to the ground floor. On the upper floors, where there were fewer shoppers, they managed to go up a down escalator, but were chased off before they could go down an up escalator.

On their way back to the express lift they passed through the school uniform department and stopped by a display of stiff velour hats sitting on the ends of sticks like large mushrooms.

'Just look at those!' exclaimed Henny. She took a green one and popped it on her head. 'How does it suit me?'

'Dreadful.' Bella took a navy one. 'At least I match.'

'Two little maids from school are we,' sang Henny, finger to chin—the song had been on television the week before.

They danced up and down, watching themselves in the long mirror.

> 'Two little maids from school are we,
> Filled to the brim with buns and tea'

'Girls! Put those hats back *at once!* Where is your mother?'

A tall lady with straight black hair and a metal brooch saying SUPERVISOR was glaring down at them.

'She's over there, behind the coats.' Bella gave her a brilliant smile.

'Buying us new uniforms,' added Henny.

The supervisor let her eyes wander over Bella's cloak and long skirt and Henny's patched jeans which had been Michael's.

'Hm!' she said, in a tone which indicated that uniforms were certainly long overdue. 'You go across there and stay with her. This is a department store, not a playground.'

They felt her eyes on their backs as they walked away.

'Silly old pig!' muttered Bella, once they were safely past the coats.

'We'd better go down anyway—they must have got that stuff by now.'

Somewhat subdued, they arrived back at the braid counter to find that their assistant had gone and a newer younger one with red hair had arrived.

Bella explained.

'Yes, that's right, she told me. She's gone to get it, but she's not back yet.' She looked at her watch. 'I think she must have stopped to have her coffee break on the way.'

'Oh! Well, can you tell us how much it's going to be?' Bella explained about the money and the change and the peanuts and the possible ice cream.

'I can't really, love, because if it's a new card it might be a different price. But I tell you what,' she bent down and winked at them, 'if you go out of the side door there and turn left, you'll find one of those new ice cream parlours that's just opened, and someone did say to me that you can get free samples all day today.'

Henny and Bella thanked her and rushed to follow her instructions.

The ice-cream shop had a blue-and-white striped blind, and was gleaming inside and out with white tiles covered with blue daisies. The window was half covered by a large poster:

'DAISY DAIRY
NEW-TASTE ICES
14 different flavours
Each one nicer
than the last!
Come in for your FREE TASTE today
and tell us which one you like best!'

'What a stroke of luck!' said Henny. 'To think we might have come yesterday and missed it all!'

'Each one nicer than the last,' read Bella. She smacked her lips. 'That sounds like my sort of shop.'

'It might just mean that they start you off on one that's really horrid,' pointed out Henny. 'Let's find out.'

'Hi there!' said the assistant. He was wearing a white peaked hat with daisies round the edge. 'And which one would you like to try?'

'We'd like to try the lot,' said Henny.

'You might *like* to,' said the man, 'but you're not going to. This is a limited offer, see, like it says.' He pointed to a printed notice at the front of the counter.

'Please choose any two
and then fill in the form.
Thank you for your
co-operation.'

'You tell me which two you want, then you try them. Then you fill in those forms, and you drop 'em in that box there. *Most* people buy another for themselves. So what's it to be?'

'Two each?'

'Yeah.'

Henny chose orange and lemon. Bella chose chocolate and strawberry.

'Though if each one was really nicer than the last, people would always like the second one more, no matter what it was,' remarked Henny.

The man grunted as he scooped half-size dollops into small paper cups and pushed them across.

'Don't forget your forms. Take 'em over there.'

They carried their ice creams over to a counter where there were pencils chained to a hook in the wall.

'They're heavenly,' said Henny.

Please choose any two
form
your

'But there's not much of them.'

'Or you *could* say, there's not much of them but they're heavenly. It depends how you look at it. Can I have a taste of yours? You can have a go at mine ... I think I like the lemon best.'

'Mmm ... the strawberry just tastes pink.'

They ate their ice creams very slowly, studying the forms.

These started off: Which ice creams did you choose? and then went on to ask questions like, Which colour did you prefer? Which flavour? Which texture? and ended with How often do you buy ice cream? Do you eat it for dessert? Are Daisy Ices good value for money?

'That's a silly question,' said Henny. 'Course they are if you don't pay for them. Still, it's only fair to fill them in. There's not a lick left in my cup.'

The two of them went down the list distributing ticks among the answers, and dropped the papers in the box.

'Thank you,' said Henny politely as they walked towards the door. The man was busy serving three businessmen with double cones and only nodded without looking at them.

'He's not a very friendly man,' said Henny, as they started walking back.

'Considering he sells something as nice as ice cream.'

'I don't suppose he'd give us two more?'

'He doesn't look the generous type.'

'It seems a shame, only trying two.'

'Four, if you count each other's.'

'Still ... that leaves ten we haven't tried.'

'Ten ... Daisy Ices might be glad if we had another go.'

'We might like the next ones lots more.'

'And it isn't as if we wouldn't do anything for it.'

'Course not. We'd get the ice cream. They'd get our opinions.'

'It's a fair exchange.'

They stopped and looked at each other.

'I expect he'd recognize us.'

'He mightn't. People don't look at kids.'

'He might though. There weren't many children came in when we were there, only very little ones with their Mums. Most of them are at school.'

'Tell you what,' said Henny. 'You take my duffle coat and tuck your skirt up. I'll put your cloak over my arm. You give me your headscarf and I'll put it on. If he's noticed us at all he's more likely to have looked at our clothes than our faces.'

With Bella's navy headscarf pulled half over her face, Henny felt quite different, and Bella, lost in Henny's duffle, looked squarer and far more substantial than her usual self.

'And you do the talking this time,' directed Henny.

The man was listening to a transistor, and hardly looked up as they came in.

'Two samples each please,' said Bella in her plummiest voice. 'One nut and one peppermint and one blackcurrant and one banana.'

The man pushed them across with his eyes on the radio. 'Take a form and fill it up, then drop it in the box.'

They carried them over to the counter and ate them gleefully, enjoying each mouthful and trying not to giggle.

'I think I really like peppermint best.'

'Blackcurrant's my favourite so far.'

'You look like a Russian peasant.'

'You look like a farmer's boy.'

'Shhh ... he'll hear us.'

They finished in silence and added their forms to the others.

'Goodbye,' said Bella graciously. Henny snorted. The man looked up, but they were gone.

'What'd you want to go and make a noise like that for?'

'I couldn't help it. Anyway, we could hardly try again ... Or could we?'

'Four and four's eight. That still leaves six we haven't tasted.'

'It seems a shame not to have a go.'

'I mean, then we'd really have a good idea of the full range, wouldn't we?'

'We'd be able to recommend them to all our friends.'

'I dare say Daisy Ices would be very pleased.'

'Mind you, even if we went back again that'd still leave two we hadn't tried.'

'Yes, but one of them's bound to be boring old vanilla. We needn't count that.'

'Still ... do you think we dare?'

They were standing on the edge of the pavement, debating, when along the street came a crocodile of green-uniformed schoolgirls with one teacher at the front and another behind.

'All right girls! We'll all stop here for a minute while Miss Pearce pops inside the store. You may talk quietly, but stay in your lines.'

'Ooh, look, Miss Partridge! Free ice creams! Do let's go in, Miss Partridge! It wouldn't take a moment! You could have one too, Miss Partridge!'

'Certainly not, girls! Out of the question. Now, Maureen, that'll do.'

Maureen subsided, muttering angrily. She was a dark gaunt girl near the back of the crocodile, who had been standing near the now absent Miss Pearce.

Henny gave Bella a twitch.

'Come on! I've got an idea.'

Henny pulled Bella towards Maureen and her partner.

'Tell you what—you two lend us your hats for a

minute and we'll get some ice cream and go halves in it. Are you on?'

Maureen looked at them suspiciously.

'What do you need our hats for?'

'It'd take too long to explain. We're not going to pinch them or anything. Look, keep this scarf till we get back.' Henny pulled off Bella's scarf and handed it over. 'But you'll have to make up your mind right away.'

Maureen looked along to the other end of the crocodile. The teacher was glancing at her watch and then at the department store across the road.

'Right!' said Maureen. She snatched off her own hat and the hat of the girl next to her. 'Wake up, Jane! But for heaven's sake be quick.'

Henny and Bella pulled the hats on and tugged them well down.

'Here goes!'

They marched into the shop side by side.

'Two samples each please,' said Henny, trying out a vaguely French accent. 'One apricot and one raspberry.'

'And one tutti frutti and one pis—pis—'

'Pistachio.' The man glanced down at their hats and then out of the window. An expression of horror dawned. 'Hey—you're not all coming in?'

'No. Just us two, 'cause we're seniors. Excuse us ...' Henny took two extra plastic spoons from the glass on the counter—'we're sharing these with our friends.'

Maureen and Jane were ducked down untying and retying their shoe laces. A ripple had run along the crocodile to the teacher in front, who was gazing back along the double row of hats behind her.

Henny and Arabella bobbed down, and Maureen and her friend yanked off their hats and replaced them on their heads.

'About time too!' Maureen stood up and shook her legs. 'I was starting to get cramp.'

'Maureen! Jane! What's going on back there?'

'Nothing, Miss Partridge. Just standing here, waiting, like you told us to.' Maureen gazed at her innocently. Miss Partridge turned away.

'Ah, good!' she exclaimed in relief. 'Here comes Miss Pearce! Now girls—put your best foot forward!'

'Hand over the ices—quick!'

'Hang on—just one spoonful each.'

Spoons flicked in and out. Into the apricot, into the pink, into the fruit, into the green. At the front, Miss Partridge and Miss Pearce, chatting, were already on the move.

'Here you are! Good luck!'

The crocodile unrolled towards the corner. Just before Maureen and Jane disappeared around it they turned and flourished their daisy-printed cups. Henny and Bella waved back.

'Pity that lot went so quickly.'

'My taste buds got thoroughly confused.'

'Still, we did it! Twelve tastes.' Bella turned and looked towards the shop. 'I think we might give the forms a miss, don't you?'

The assistant was leaning over his counter and staring at them with what, even from a distance, looked like dawning recognition.

'I agree,' said Henny. 'I think Daisy Ices have heard the last of us for today.'

Putting their heads down, they turned away and crossed the road back to the store.

'Gosh, it's late!' said Bella guiltily, as they passed through the clock department. 'I hope she's got the braid all ready.'

'Wherever have you been?' asked the first assistant. 'I thought you must have given up and gone home.' She looked at them with a puzzled frown. 'You *are* the ones for the cream braid, aren't you? You look different somehow.'

'Oh!' said Bella. She tugged down her skirt and took off Henny's coat. The lady handed over a small package and raised her eyebrows. Henny and Bella, deciding against explanations, thanked her politely and left to count the change.

'My goodness me!' said Jessica Roach, looking up from her sewing-machine. 'You took your time, darlings, didn't you?'

'We had to wait for *ages*, Jessica.' Bella put the small packet down on the table, and explained about the damaged braid. 'We had to keep going back and back, but it's all there now. Except for the change, because we spent that on some peanuts because you said we could.'

'So I suppose you're feeling quite full up and don't want anything to eat?' said Mrs Roach, teasing, as she leaned down to switch off her machine.

'Oh, that was *hours* ago!' said Bella. 'We've had a whole long bus ride since.'

'And we've had a very busy morning,' added Henny. 'There's something about holidays that always makes you hungry.'

4

The Christmas Raffle

It had been a cold wet miserable morning and it was a cold wet miserable afternoon.

Everyone had been in a bad temper all day. Henny, hurrying home with her head down to keep the rain out of her eyes, thought that it didn't feel in the least bit Christmassy. She hadn't even enjoyed practising the carols for the Nativity play. Miss Yarrow had come to school with a cold and could only croak, and without her voice singing them into enthusiasm everything had seemed very flat and dull.

As she turned into the main road the pavement at her feet glistened with rectangles of light from the shop windows she was passing. She could see the blurred outlines of the shadows of baubles and wreaths hanging in the baker's and the greengrocer's and the small supermarket, and knew that if she turned her head sideways she would see the holly-framed posters in the windows—*Season's Greetings to All Our Friends* and *A Merry Yuletide to One and All*—but she refused to look and went on plodding along the pavement, watching her shadow swallow up the other shadows as she passed.

Henny snuffled. Her nose was cold, her hands were cold, even her inside was cold. And she still had no idea what she was going to do about Christmas presents.

When she turned off into Linden Road the wind stopped playing with the rain and instead flung handfuls of tiny stinging hailstones. Henny started to run, skidding and almost falling on a plastic bag which had blown into an icy puddle.

By the time she reached the front door she felt chilled and miserable right through. There was no light spilling out on the front step. No sounds from inside; no radio, no television, no voices. For once, of course, she had got there first. She rang the bell and banged uselessly on the door. As she expected, nothing happened and no one came.

She pulled herself tightly against the door and wedged herself into the corner farthest from the wind. She stared accusingly down the road, practising her grumbles in her head.

She had no chance to use them. When Michael turned up five minutes later he was dragging along a Jack crying so loudly that Henny's rehearsed complaints were totally drowned.

'All right, Jack. Shut up!' Michael dragged the key out on the string round his neck, shuddering as the icy rain blew into the exposed gap. 'We'll all be inside in a moment!'

The door swung open and Henny fumbled for the switch.

It was warmer inside, but not much. Jack was still sobbing at the top of his voice, and there was a general air of desolation.

Michael kicked the door shut behind him.

'About time too.' He sighed heavily, and started to drag Jack along the hallway.

'What's up with *him*? It's not like Jack to go on like that.'

'He tripped and fell into a puddle down by the *British Queen*. He didn't look where he was going. His trousers are soaked and so are his shoes. Shut up or I'll *clobber* you, Jack!'

Jack's wails redoubled. The narrow hall was full of noise.

For a moment Michael looked as if he was about to carry out his threat. Instead, he bent down and undid Jack's anorak and yanked it off, then he squatted on the floor and undid his shoes. They squelched loudly as he pulled them off.

'Oh, well, I suppose he can't help it,' he said resignedly. 'His feet are like ice. Tell you what, Henny, run a bath and shove him in. I'll go and put the kettle on and we'll all feel better.'

Henny felt rebellious. Her toes were freezing too *and* she'd had to wait outside for absolutely ages. But Michael had vanished into the kitchen before she'd decided whether it was worth staging a full-scale protest.

Anyway Michael was right. By the time they heard their mother's key in the front door Jack was his usual cheerful self again, wrapped cosily in his twice-handed-down bright blue dressing-gown. The three of them, with cups of tea and biscuits, were watching a ski-ing adventure on television, and the rattle of the hail on the windows and the sight of piles of snow on the film made them feel warmer and snugger than ever.

'Well!' exlaimed Mrs Cary, opening the door, 'talk about snug as a bug in a rug!' Henny slid off her chair and ran to give her a quick hug.

'You should have seen us earlier though! Especially Jack. He was *dripping*. I put his things in the kitchen on the back of the chair. What about you, Mum? Your shoes look soaked as well. I'll get your slippers.'

'Would you, love? Thank you. Oh, dear, what a day!' She took off her shoes and padded down the hallway, leaving damp footprints on the lino. Henny cast a lingering gaze at the screen, where a storm was threatening to bury a mountain chalet, and went to fetch her mother's slippers from under the bathroom stool.

They were busy chatting in the kitchen while Mrs

Cary conjured a meal together—at least Henny chatted, and her mother made friendly grunts and nods—when the front bell rang.

'Whoever can it be out in weather like this?' said Mrs Cary. They listened. There was no sound of Michael running to the door. The bell rang again.

'You go, Henny. It's always the same. Either you all rush at once or no one goes at all.'

Henny opened the front door the smallest bit possible, to keep the cold outside where it belonged. The rain and the hail had stopped, but the wind poured through the crack.

'Oh, hello, Mr Marston.' It was the old man from next door. He had a dark blue woollen scarf wrapped round and round his neck. 'Come in.'

'No, thanks, love. Your Mum'll be busy with your tea, and she won't be wanting me under her feet. I only popped round to give you this. The postman left it with me this morning. Got lots of them foreign stamps on. I was waiting for the rain to stop to bring it round. What weather, eh? Let's hope it changes before Christmas, makes you feel really low, dunnit? Here you are then. Let's hope it's worth waiting for. Cheerio.'

Henny took the parcel he thrust through the gap and stood for a moment studying it as she shut the door.

'Who was it?' called Mrs Cary.

'Mr Marston with a parcel.'

She walked slowly down the hallway, turning it over. It was a large oblong parcel wrapped in brown paper. On the front it was addressed in big black capitals to MICHAEL, PENELOPE, AND JOHN D. CARY. On the back there was a large pale green label and on it writing in the same black pen in words she couldn't understand. Underneath was the name of the sender. It was scrawled and the ink had run, but she didn't need to read it to know where the parcel had come from.

The livingroom door sprang open. There was a sudden blare of music.

'A parcel?' said Jack, bouncing towards her. 'For me?'

'A parcel?' said Michael. 'Bags of gold? I could just do with some.'

'A parcel?' said Mum, putting a lid on a saucepan and turning round from the stove. 'What sort of parcel?'

'A parcel from Dad,' said Henny. Her mother turned back to the stove and lit the gas under another pan.

'Is it a present?' said Jack. 'Can I open it? Can I open it right away?'

'Perhaps it's Christmas presents,' said Henny.

'It's ages too soon for Christmas,' said Michael.

'Go on!' said Jack, 'Let's open it! Let *me* open it!'

'I tell you what,' said Mrs Cary, turning to take the parcel from Henny. '*I'll* open it. Then if what's inside is wrapped in Christmas paper, we'll keep it. And if it isn't, well, then you'll see anyway, won't you?'

She put the parcel on the table, took down the kitchen scissors and cut her way through the sticky tape and paper. Michael, Henny and Jack clustered round and watched.

Inside the paper was a cardboard box.

And inside the box were three other boxes—unwrapped—with their names written on them in the same black ink.

Jack's was bright yellow, with a picture on it in red and black. Inside was a silver gun with fancy patterns sticking out of a brown and red holster.

'Gosh!' said Jack. His eyes glowed.

Michael's box was smaller and plainer. Inside was a black leather belt with curling designs running along it, with a buckle made of two snakes twining round each other.

'Neat, man!'

Henny's was much the largest of the three—gold cardboard with a thick transparent sheet for a lid. Inside was a doll with curling black hair and bright red lips. It had an elaborate lace head-dress falling over its pale face, and an embroidered apron over layers of brightly coloured skirts and petticoats. In one hand it held a bunch of tiny flowers. Its bright black eyes gazed steadily over Henny's left shoulder.

Henny's eyes met her mother's across the table.

'Well, it isn't easy when he hasn't seen you for so long ...'

'And plenty of girls do like dolls. I mean, Susan does ... and so does Tracy ...'

'You can stand it up next to the one you got last year.'

Henny nodded; not pointing out that it would be a tight squeeze to fit anything more into the half room that was hers.

'Well, supper's almost ready,' said Mrs Cary, briskly. 'Do you want the stamps, Henny? Cut them off and take them away, then put the paper in the bin. Michael, you set the table. Jack, if you don't stop saying bang bang I'll take that away from you.'

Supper over, and Jack banished to bed, Michael sat at one end of the table groaning over some maths homework. Henny sat at the other end bent over a piece of paper. Mrs Cary, shutting the door on Jack, came into the kitchen to retrieve her cup of tea. She yawned.

'I think I'll go and flop down for a bit. What are you frowning at, Henny? Something for school?'

'It's an ideas list.'

'What sort of an ideas list?'

'For Christmas presents. Time's getting on.'

Henny's mother moved behind her. Henny wasn't quite quick enough in covering up the paper on which she had written *Ways of Making Money for Xmas presents*.

'Henny, love! Don't worry about that, now. We're not expecting anything grand and fancy and shop-bought. Are we, Mike? You can make us some of your super pictures, and that'll be great. Come on—put it away and let's go and play a game. How about Pelmanism? Or Monopoly?'

Henny shook her head.

'No, I'd rather get on with this, thanks. Don't worry, Mum. I'm not going to rob a bank or anything.'

'You'd look pretty daft if your tried,' said Michael, looking up. 'I can just see you with Jack's gun. Bang bang! Hands up! Your money or your life!'

'*My* ideas are practical,' said Henny with dignity.

'Your ideas are ingenious,' said her mother warily. 'But ... Well, as long as I see them first.'

'*No*, Mum! That would spoil everything,' said Henny. 'Presents should be surprises. And getting them shouldn't bother the people you're trying to surprise. Tell you what,' she offered, 'I'll show them to Mike.'

'All right. As long as it doesn't end in fights.'

'You run along and sit down quietly, Mum. We won't do anything daft.'

Michael was only too glad to abandon his own problems for someone else's, and reached over for Henny's paper.

'Let's have a look then.'

Henny gave up her piece of paper reluctantly. She wasn't in the mood for any of Mike's funny remarks. It was all very well to talk of making things, but she knew exactly what she wanted to get her mother for Christmas, and it simply wasn't anything she could make herself. She was going to get her a new egg beater. A splendid new rotary beater that went round and round whizz whizz whizz and never sulked and jammed and spread batter all over the kitchen.

Mrs Cary's beater had been a wedding present, and it had been getting more and more temperamental every time it was used. Henny knew her mother would never buy another until it actually fell to pieces. And then she'd like to get her something pretty as well—not just useful ... And she had ideas for Michael too, and even Jack ...

'Idea Number 1. Go round and polish things,' read Mike. 'What does that mean?'

'It means what it says,' said Henny tartly. 'I could go round to other people's houses and polish things for them. I'm good at polishing. Mum says so. I could polish anything they wanted me to. Doorknockers and letterboxes and trays and things. I wouldn't mind how much I polished as long as I got paid for it. I like seeing things shine anyway.'

'I don't think Mum would like you going round knocking at just anyone's door ... No, all right, Henny, I don't *know*. Let me read the next bit ...

'Idea Number 2. Take dogs for walks. Most of the people round here take out their own dogs, don't they? And you're still on the small side, Henny. I can't see anyone lending you their alsatians. Supposing you ended up with a nasty yapping dog, like Muffin down the road?'

'There is that,' agreed Henny reluctantly. 'But the next one is a really great idea, one of my best.'

'Shut up kids,' read Michael. He read it again. 'Shut up kids. What on earth are you on about?'

'I thought I could go round shutting up kids—little ones like Jack.'

'What in? Cupboards?'

'Don't be daft! Looking after them, like I do with Jack when Mum's busy. Not babysitting exactly. More keeping them out of their Mum's hair while they get on with making mince pies and Christmas pud. I bet they'd be glad to pay for a bit of peace and quiet.'

'Yes, but all the babies you know have got older brothers and sisters already—that's why you know them. You'd have to get hold of some babies that don't have any.'

'I could advertise. I could put a card in the shop down the road. 'Get ready for Christmas in peace and quiet. Your baby (or toddler) entertained by an expert. Games played. Castles built for knocking down. Years of experience. No job too small!' I bet I'd have hundreds of replies.'

'Henny, there *aren't* hundreds of babies round here. And even if there were I don't suppose their Mums would be all that happy leaving their darlings with someone they didn't know.'

'You're a real wet blanket, Mike! A soggy, soggy blanket! I bet you'll say something nasty about Idea Number 4 as well!'

'Make flapjacks and sell them,' read Michael slowly.

'You know I can do it! Mum's helped me make them for the last two bring-and-buys. I can do it all by myself now. And they're good, you know that—you ate enough of the last lot!'

'Yes, but Henny, if you want to make boxes and boxes of flapjacks you'll need masses of stuff to make it with, and I don't think Mum can afford that, not with Christmas coming.'

'It's not fair!' Henny's eyes filled with tears. She stared down at the table so Michael shouldn't see. 'I've been saving my pocket money for *weeks*, but it just isn't enough, and everything I think of you tell me won't work.'

Michael looked at Number 5. 'Sell Jokes to Comics.' And Number 6, 'Buy Premium Bond when I can afford it and Win a Fortune.' He said nothing. From the living-room they could hear the distant wail of violins.

'Tell you what, Henny,' he said suddenly. 'That doll. You know—the one you just got. Why don't you sell it?'

'Oh, Mike, do you think I could? It doesn't seem right somehow, selling a present.'

'I don't see why. In soppy stories girls are always

selling things to raise money for their starving families, and then it's a Noble Deed.'

'It would be a Noble Deed if I really wanted the doll,' Henny pointed out. 'But as I don't ... do you think I ought to ask Mum?'

'I don't see why. It's your present, isn't it? If you want to sell it, I wouldn't bother Mum about it. Besides, if you sold the doll it would be better than having it just sitting there getting dustier and dustier like last year's, and the year before's.'

'It'd be a waste really, wouldn't it? Someone like Tracy would love a doll like that, she's got about six already ... And it's not as though I was going to go out and blow the whole lot on cream buns or anything.' Henny's depression vanished. Her mind skated rapidly over various potential buyers. 'The only thing is, how do you think I ought to sell it? Just go round and ask people, one by one? And how much do you think I can charge?'

'*I* don't know. How should I know how much dolls cost? How much do you need?'

'Heaps and heaps. £4.00? £5.00?'

'That sounds an awful lot. Can anyone afford that? Besides, people don't want to give that much when they're buying something secondhand.'

'Secondhand? I haven't even opened the box.'

'No, but you know what I mean. If something costs as much as it might from a shop, people would rather go to a shop and be able to choose something themselves.'

'I know! I'll *raffle* it! It'll probably be much easier to sell raffle tickets at a few pence than to get anyone to fork out pounds all at once.'

'Hang on!' said Michael. 'For once maths comes in useful. How much could you sell your tickets for?'

'A penny? Two pence?'

'Think, Henny! If you sell tickets for a penny each you'd have to sell 100 before you even got a pound.'

'Twenty pence then. And then if I sold 100 at twenty pence I'd get £20.00. Cor!'

'Well, you're not likely to sell 100 at twenty pence, are you? In fact, you mightn't sell *any* at that price.'

Henny counted up. 'There's Tracy, and Susan, and Rhona, and Bella and Kim and Theresa, and Sharon ... mmmm ... say ten, perhaps twelve in my class, perhaps more, because some of the boys might buy some for their little sisters ... And in the other classes, the girls I know ... say twenty, twenty-five.'

'So if you're right you might sell anything from ten to thirty or so. Or more, or less, of course.' Mike was getting interested. It was a lot more practical than his homework. 'I think twenty pence is too much.'

'Tickets are mostly five pence at bring-and-buys,' volunteered Henny. 'Mind, I've never won anything yet.'

'If you sold thirty at five pence you'd only get £1.50.'

'But if I sold sixty I'd get £3.00. And if I sold more I'd get even more.'

'And if you sold less you'd get less. It's a risk.'

'I'll take it!' Henny was flushed with enthusiasm. She already saw herself walking into the ironmonger's and buying the best eggbeater she could find. 'I can't lose anything, can I? And some people might buy lots. I'll ask five pence and four for fifteen pence. That sounds all right, doesn't it?'

'I hope so,' said Michael, remembering some of the difficulties Henny's schemes had produced in the past. Still, there didn't seem to be anything that *could* go wrong with this one. Anyway the sound of the front room door opening and shutting reminded him of the three sums he had yet to answer.

It was still grey and miserable when Henny woke up the next morning, but she was sure that it was going to be a great improvement on the day before. Today she was going to organize the best raffle ever. She'd decided against making her own tickets. It looked more official if you had the proper ones.

She took some of her pocket money savings out of the pink papier-mâché money-box pig she had made last year at school, and at the paper-shop she found the right sort of book with pale green slips inside.

When she got into the classroom she crossed out *Cloakroom Tickets* and wrote in bright red *Fantastic Doll Raffle*. She had to write small to get it in, and the result was less impressive than she'd hoped. She turned the book over and wrote on the blank back—'Your Chance to Win!!!'

Kim and Bella peered over her shoulders.

'What doll?'

'What raffle?'

Henny explained.

Arabella glanced round the room.

'I wouldn't let Sir see,' she said.

'Whyever not? There's nothing wrong. It's my doll, honest. I can do what I like with it.'

'Of course it is,' said Bella. 'It's not that. It's the raffle bit.'

'What's wrong with that? The school runs raffles. I heard Miss Yarrow say that we make almost as much out of raffles as the rest of the stalls put together.'

'I don't know why, but I feel there's something funny about raffles. Something to do with getting special permission from the council or something. I heard Miss talking about it last year.'

'Anyway, *I* don't see nothing wrong with it. What's this fantastic doll like, anyway?'

Henny described it.

But what Bella had said left her with an uneasy feeling. There were so many excellent things that you weren't allowed to do, from walking barefoot to school in the rain to selling lemonade outside your house. She decided to take Bella's advice. It was a nuisance, though.

Trade was slower than she had hoped, but by the end of the day she had found fifteen doll lovers who thought they might buy tickets, six who said they definitely would, and two—Bella and Theresa—who actually bought four and paid for them.

Next day she brought a bag to school she could sling round her neck in which to put the ticket stubs and all the money she was going to collect.

She spent all her playtimes and her dinner break going round to yesterday's clients. Only four of the positives had actually remembered and brought cash, but, to compensate, eight of the uncertains had decided in favour. By school-leaving time she had collected ninety-five pence.

The next day went well too, but the day after that she sold only four more tickets. It was true that her bag was getting heavier, and she was certainly much better off than before her raffle had started, but she was still well short of the target she'd set herself.

'Come on, Henny,' Theresa said impatiently as they walked back into class for afternoon school. 'When's the draw going to be then? It's three whole days since I bought my tickets.'

'Ssh!' Henny looked round to make sure Mr Fielding hadn't heard. 'Give me a little bit longer. There's quite a few people who haven't made their minds up yet.'

'Why don't you bring it to school and let's all have a look? I might buy another ticket myself. My mum gave me five pence last night for cleaning out the grates.'

'That's a good idea—I will. I thought of bringing it before, but it's been so wet I didn't want to spoil it. It's a real beauty, you wait and see.'

Next day was crisp, cold and sunny. Henny, fetching

a plastic bag from the kitchen, paused for a moment to admire the way the sun made the doll's black curls gleam, glinted on the richly coloured silks of her skirts, picked out the delicate white lace on the collar. Even the little bunch of flowers she held looked almost alive. Surely the sight of her would make lots of people flock to buy tickets!

She was right.

When she arrived in the playground and opened the bag to reveal her sleeping beauty, she was surrounded. Before they went into the classroom she had sold eleven more tickets; and there were many more firm promises that money would definitely be brought after the weekend.

Henny went into the classroom feeling on top of the world. It was great to see the sun after so much rain; they would sing carols first thing; and with the money she'd saved, and the money she already had in her bag, and what was promised to her, she would be able to buy a very splendid beater. She knew just what she wanted. She'd seen it in the Co-op. She'd even been in to give it a test spin. And she might have enough to buy something for Michael and Jack.

'Henny, you haven't brought something else to school have you?' asked Mr Fielding, in a long-suffering voice. 'It's time you started taking things home, not bringing more here!'

'It's all right, Sir. I'm taking it back tonight. It's only for today.'

Henny took the doll out of her bag and piled three boxes on top of each other to make room to stand it on the window sill. It smiled out across the class.

'She's certainly very handsome. I suppose she's new and you can't bear to be parted from her.'

Mr Nicholas turned to pick up his register.

'Oh, yes, she can, Sir.' said a loud voice. 'That's a prize. A prize for her raffle.'

'A prize?' said Mr Fielding, turning back. 'What raffle?'

'Henny's raffle, Sir. Didn't you know?' Stephen Blake gazed innocently at Mr Fielding.

'A raffle?' said Mr Fielding again. 'Come here, Henny.'

Henny left her seat by the window and walked nervously to the front of the class. Steve smiled sweetly at her as she passed.

'Now what's all this about?' said Mr Fielding quietly, sitting down behind his desk. 'Are you really running a raffle?'

'Yes, but it's my doll, really it is, Sir, I can do what I like with it, and ...'

'I'm sorry, Henny, but you can't raffle it. I'm sure it's your doll, and you didn't mean any harm, but it's against the law. Don't interrupt me, please. Have you sold any tickets? Do you know who you've sold them to? I'm sorry, but you'll have to give everybody back their money. You understand? *Everybody*.'

'I can't! I can't! I've spent every single moment of every single playtime this week raffling the doll. I'm not doing any harm. I didn't make anybody buy one if they didn't want to. I can't give it all back. Why should I? I don't see ...'

'Henny, that'll do! Sit down and calm down. The rest of the day you go round and do exactly as I say. I'm not arguing with you.'

Henny went back to her seat on the point of tears. Only the sight of Steve's blue eyes and satisfied face kept her from shedding them.

Break was misery. The sun still shone, and the air was crisp, and the playground full of people playing, but she was filled with wretchedness.

The only bright side was that it was much quicker to give money back than it had been to get it. By the time the bell rang for afternoon lessons her little bag was almost empty.

As she walked back towards her desk, and saw her doll leaning against the window, she remembered all her work and hopes. She couldn't help it. The sobs she had been choking down all morning rose to her throat.

To her horror tears began to fall.

'That's what you get for meddling in what's none of your business.'

Steve's voice was so soft that no one but Henny heard; but Mr Fielding caught sight of his face as he spoke.

'Henny,' he said.

Henny couldn't speak. She jerked her head.

'Henny. Come here a moment, please.'

Henny walked up to the desk.

'Have you done as I said?'

Henny nodded her head.

'I'm sorry I had to insist. But it is against the law to run raffles, and if anybody heard about yours the school would get into trouble. You wouldn't want that, would you?'

Henny slowly shook her head.

'But the school ...' she tried to get the words out.

'Yes, I know the school runs raffles. But they have to get special permission, and it's always for a charity. What was your charity, Henny? Can you tell me?'

Slowly Henny explained about Christmas presents, and the doll's arrival, and Michael's idea, and what she had been planning.

Mr Fielding listened thoughtfully. His eyes roamed over the rest of the room, daring them to create a disturbance, and came to rest on Steve.

'Tell me,' he said, 'How much did your raffle bring in?'

'£2.90,' said Henny. 'And six people promised faithfully to bring money on Monday. I've still got ten pence left in my bag. Valerie Stacey's away today.'

'Well, then I tell you what. I've got a little girl of my own, you know.'

'You have?' Henny looked at him in astonishment. She had never thought of Sir as a father.

'Yes. Oh, much smaller than you—only three. But she loves dolls, and I'm sure she'd like yours. Now, what would you say if I offered to buy yours for—let's say £3.50. Does that seem like a good idea?'

'Oh, Sir! If you really want to. But don't you think ...' she remembered the havoc Jack had caused in the past, '... that perhaps she might spoil it? Being so little, I mean? I wouldn't want you to pay all that and then have it spoilt.'

'Maybe we'll just let her look at it for a bit. Don't you worry. It's a deal then?'

'It's a deal!'

Henny, eyes sparkling, walked past her seat to collect the doll. She didn't look at Steve, or say a word. She returned and put the doll on the desk.

'Thank you, Henny.' Mr Fielding took out his wallet and counted three notes and a 50p piece. 'These are for you. But I think I should keep them until the end of the day. And look here,' he took the cover off the box and plucked the small bunch of flowers from the doll's elegant hands, 'take these. My little Anne would simply lose them. You could put them in a tiny pot at home to remind you of your present.'

Henny, twisting the little bunch of flowers between her fingers, returned to her desk. The afternoon sun came through the windows from a clear frost-blue sky.

Suddenly, it felt like Christmas.

5
The Spring Fair

'Are you going to make something for the Spring Fair, Mum?'

Mrs Cary looked up from the pocket she was mending on Jack's anorak.

'It *can't* be the Spring Fair yet! It is no time since the Christmas Bring-and-Buy! And it isn't the least little bit like spring. It's far colder than it was in January. I feel I'm waking up in a fridge every morning.'

'It's not till the end of the week. I expect they didn't know it was going to go on being so cold when they fixed the date. It's earlier this year because Theresa's Mum—you know, the one who runs the refreshments—is going away. She's going to Ireland for a long holiday and her Gran's Golden Wedding. Lots of Mums have been coming on Tuesday afternoons to sew things, but I told them you couldn't because you were out all day in an office. We're all supposed to be making things too.'

'What sort of things?'

'I made a pin cushion in sewing, and I started on a purse, only it got left on the window-sill and Steve spilt paint on it. He said it was an accident but you can bet it wasn't. I didn't mind really. It was a boring bit of material and I was getting fed up with it. It's not fair, all the girls are making things themselves, and all the boys are saying they can't and getting their Mums to make things for them! Well, not *all* of them. Mark's made an everlasting calendar out of a box and lots of cards he cut out and put months and numbers on, and Kevin's made a toy boat out of bits of wood and painted it red, but Dennis's mother is making sausage dogs ...'

'*Sausage* dogs?'

'Yes, you know—to put against the door when it's draughty. And David's Mum is making lavender bags, and George's Mum said she might be able to knit a tea cosy when she was on night duty ...' Henny sighed. 'I think I'll make another pin cushion. It doesn't take all that long, and I like putting the pins in afterwards. In my last one I stuck them in to say HELP!'

Mrs Cary threaded her needle again.

'Well, Henny, I wish I could help *you*, but by the time we've eaten, and Jack's in bed, and I've caught up with the ironing and mending ... What did I do last year?'

'You made two fruit cakes. Not exactly fruit cakes, but sort of.'

'I remember, Great-Aunt Dorothy's recipe for an Irish fruit loaf. We ate one and I gave the other to the Fair.'

'Mrs Murphy—Theresa's Mum you know—said oh good, she hadn't seen those for ages, and instead of putting them on the cake stall she sliced them up and buttered them and sold them with the refreshments. She said they'd get more money that way, but *I* think it was because she wanted a taste herself and she could hardly nibble bits off the end, could she? It went ever so quickly.'

'I wonder why I haven't made it since ...? I know, you have to soak the fruit overnight, and I never seem to think that far ahead. I wonder if I can still find the recipe?'

She cut the thread and stuck her needle in the fish-shaped pin cushion with the non-matching buttons for eyes which Henny had made for her two Christmases ago, and went to search through the large envelope in which she kept odd recipes and hints and coupons.

'Dear me, I could throw half this stuff away ... Send in before November 1st ... Valid until June 30th and that was the year *before* last ... Ah! Got it! Now, what do we need? Flour, tea, sugar, egg ... that's all right. Dried fruit—I finished all that off at Christmas. I'll buy some more tomorrow, Henny, if I remember. I'm not promising, mind, but I'll try. I'll stick the recipe up here on the shelf to remind me. Now off to bed with you. There's still plenty of time before Friday.'

Monday was a day of sleet and grey skies, and a mean east wind blew crisp papers and chicken boxes along the street. At school the daffodil bulbs by the window got shrivelled brown tips, and at home the rock-hard margarine fought against the toast.

Mrs Cary came back late on Monday and late again on Tuesday. The recipe sat on the shelf; and Henny, watching her mother flop back and kick off wet shoes, decided to put off mentioning the cake until a better moment.

On Wednesday the wind dropped and the sleet vanished. The sky turned a cold, brilliant blue and the playground was covered all day long with glittering flecks of frost, like powdered glass.

Henny ran back from school, but even though she was wearing the bright red gloves her Granny Lindsay had knitted her for Christmas, her hands grew so cold and numb that it almost hurt to ring the front door bell.

'I'm frozen right down to my toe nails,' she said, pushing past Michael and rushing for the haven of the kitchen. 'It hasn't been as cold as this for years and years. Not since the Ice Age, probably.'

'Jack was almost crying by the time we got home. Trouble is, he can't move fast enough, especially when he's got those boots on and it's as slippery as it is today. He keeps skidding and falling over. I made us a great big pot of tea to keep us going.'

'Show me to it!' Henny pulled off her shoes and rubbed her toes until they started to tingle, and then wrapped her hands gratefully round the mug of milky tea Michael pushed across the table to her.

'I agree with Mum, it doesn't feel one bit like the weather for a Spring Fair,' she said. 'I hope people come. At least it's warmer in school than outside, so perhaps they'll pop in for a cup of tea. And then they'll stop and buy. I hope. If no one picks my pin cushions I shall be very wounded. Where's Jack?'

'I told him to go and get his slippers. I suppose I'd better see what he's up to.'

The kitchen was very quiet. Through the window the outside looked black and forbidding. Henny got up and dragged her chair across so that she could stand on it and pull down the blind. Often they didn't bother, but tonight she wanted to feel snug. As she got down from the window her elbow struck the teapot. It rocked unsteadily and made her catch a quick breath of alarm.

Then a thought struck her. She pulled off the tea cosy, lifted the lid and peered inside. The hot fragrant steam rose and tickled her nose.

Yes. There was still a good cup left in the pot.

She replaced the lid and the cosy and jumped off the chair.

'What're you doing?' asked Michael suspiciously, reappearing at the door with Jack at his heels.

'Pulling down the blind,' said Henny. 'Do you want any more tea?'

'I've had two cups already. And Jack's had his—enough to warm up his milk, anyway. *And* he's had two honey sandwiches and the last bit of Sunday's cake. We're going to watch television. You coming?'

'In a minute. I'll just finish my tea.'

Henny waited until she heard the front-room door close. She wasn't going to do anything wrong, but you never knew with brothers. It was only common sense to avoid arguments.

She took the recipe from under the cream jug on the shelf, then sat down on the chair to decipher it. Luckily, Great-Aunt Dorothy's writing was not the usual grown-up scrawl, and Henny managed to read it with only an occasional puzzled pause.

She read it through twice to be sure, but it seemed quite straightforward.

> Take 2 cups of mixed dried fruit
> 1 cup leftover tea from pot
> 1 cup soft brown sugar
> Mix together and leave overnight.

She stopped reading, and checked back.

'*Two cups of mixed dried fruit.*' That was all right. Her mother had bought the fruit on Sunday when she went out to buy bread. It was in the cupboard next to the cornflakes. '*One cup soft brown sugar.*' There was brown sugar in the top cupboard well out of Jack's way—he had it when Mrs Cary had time to make him porridge for breakfast. '*One cup leftover tea.*' And that was on the draining-board waiting in the pot.

Easy.

She wondered for a moment what sort of cup to take, decided that it probably didn't matter as long as she used the same one for everything, and chose the mug Michael had given her last Easter. It had red rabbits round the side and a yellow chicken pecking at the handle.

In five minutes she had put the fruit, the sugar, and, carefully, the tea into the basin—though by now it was only just hot and no longer scalding. She stirred it round and round with the largest wooden spoon, and watched the pale gold of the sugar disappearing into the dark brown of the tea. She picked out some raisins and a couple of currants and chewed them slowly. It was a delicious recipe. It seemed almost a shame to have to cook it.

She covered it with a plate, climbed back on her chair, and put it on to the highest shelf she could reach. There were only a few bits of fruit left over in the packet, so she pulled out the bag from inside and screwed it up and tucked it in her pocket for break next day. Finally she put back the recipe under the jug. It wouldn't do to lose it now.

She hadn't intended to keep the started-off-fruit-loaf a secret from her mother, but when she came in later so cold and hungry, and Jack made so much fuss about how he'd bruised himself when he slid over at school, Henny's head was so full of the television programme she'd been watching that thoughts of her baking went right out of her head.

It wasn't until she found the leftover currants and raisins at school next day that she remembered the bowl on the shelf.

'I hope Mum gets back in time to finish it off,' she said to Bella, as she shared out the scraps of candied peel.

'Why don't you do it yourself?' asked Bella licking her fingers.

'I'm not allowed to light the oven.'

'Couldn't Michael do it for you?'

'I suppose so. He might say I ought to wait for Mum, though.'

'Not if you got it all mixed and ready before you asked him. Think of all the bother you'd be saving her. I bet she won't have time after she gets back. Jessica never has.'

'I'll see. I only read the recipe quickly. If it's easy, I'll do it, and if it's not, I'll leave it.'

It *was* easy. Henny read it twice to make sure.

Add
3 cups flour
1 lightly beaten egg
Mix and divide into two.
Put in greased standard loaf tins, and
bake for about 1 hour at gas No. 4.

What could be easier than that? Michael had gone round the corner to get some bread, and Henny felt sure she could finish the mixing before he got back.

She climbed up and got down the bowl.

'What you doing?' Jack looked up from his boiled egg.

'Baking,' said Henny importantly. She lifted the half-full jar of flour off the shelf, and broke an egg into a cup.

'*I* want to bake too.'

'Finish your tea first.'

She beat the egg with a fork and measured out the flour. There was only just room for it in the bowl—it was lucky she'd picked a large one. She made a hollow in the middle with her wooden spoon and poured in the egg. Then she started to stir. It was harder work than she expected, because she could only use one hand while she held on to the basin with the other. But bit by bit the white mound began to be swallowed up by the sticky brown tide which surrounded it.

'All gone.' Jack pushed his crushed empty eggshell away. '*My* turn to bake now.'

'All right. Just a short go, mind.'

She pushed the bowl towards Jack.

He seized the wooden spoon in both hands.

'Pat-a-cake pat-a-cake baker's MAN!' He lifted the spoon and brought it down splat! on the brown gooey mix. Sticky splatters flew up and decorated their face and hair with a plague of spots.

'You stupid boy! Now look what you've done!'

FLOUR
SA

Henny grabbed back the spoon and snatched the bowl out of reach.

Jack's mouth turned down.

'Only wanted to be a baker's man,' he mourned.

Henny heard the front door key turn in the lock, and reached for the tea towel.

'Henny, what *are* you up to? I can't leave you for five minutes. Just look at Jack's face!'

'Just look at mine!' Henny threw down the towel in disgust. 'Yuk! I feel as though I've been sprayed with syrup. I'll get a flannel—it's all his fault anyway.'

'Irish fruit loaf,' read Michael, as Henny came back from the bathroom. 'Did Mum say you could make this?'

'Not *exactly*. She was going to make it herself, but she hasn't had time, and the Fair's tomorrow, so I'm helping.'

'Mmm.' Michael took the flannel from Henny and began to scrub Jack's face with spiralling movements, as though he was polishing a metal tray. Henny carried on with her mixing. 'Well, I suppose it's all right. Anyway, you've done it now, haven't you?'

'I've just got to put it in the tins.' She started to look for them in the bottom of the cupboard. Clatter! Crash! Bang! Jack clapped his hands over his ears. Even though she pulled all the tins out on the floor, Henny could only find one loaf tin. Never mind—the small round cake tin would do just as well.

She took them over and greased them with a folded margarine paper from the fridge.

'Will you light the oven for me, Michael? Please, Michael?'

'All right. How long are they going to take?'

Henny began to divide the mixture between the tins.

'About an hour, it says. But I've got to let the oven warm first.'

'You'd better set the timer then, or you're bound to forget.'

Henny shut the oven door with a sense of triumph, and turned the hand on the clock.

'There!' she said with satisfaction. 'Now all we have to do is wait.'

'What's that gorgeous smell?' Mrs Cary wrinkled her nose as she came wearily into the kitchen, rubbing her cold hands together. 'It's certainly a whole lot nicer in than out!'

'It's a fruit loaf, Mum. *Two* fruit loaves, in fact. And they're nearly ready. I did want to keep peeping, but Michael said I shouldn't because it would let the hot air out. I'm going to have a look in five minutes' time, and I've got the wire tray all ready to put them on. It's the very first baking I've done all on my own.'

'Oh, Henny, I forgot all about it, didn't I? It's been such a week. Did you manage the spaghetti all right?'

'Yes, Michael did it. It was super. We were ever so hungry but we're not now, you go and take your coat off and then you can watch me take the tins out of the oven.'

'I'll do it, Henny. You might burn yourself. I'll be back in a moment.'

There was a hush of expectancy as Mrs Cary opened the oven door. Henny hopped up and down just behind her, and Jack stood to one side watching large-eyed with his thumb in his mouth. Even Michael had left the model he was working on to come and sniff. A waft of hot sweet air drifted out and filled the kitchen.

Mrs Cary took out the loaf tin and turned it upside down over the wire tray.

Out fell a black-studded dark brown flat oblong.

Henny stared at it in disbelief.

'But that's not a loaf! I don't believe it! I did everything just exactly as it said! I did, truly! What about the other one?'

Silently Mrs Cary reached again into the oven.

Out of the round tin clattered a black-studded dark brown disc.

Henny burst into tears.

'It's not fair! Mouldy Great-Aunt Dorothy's written down her recipe wrong, that's what! I didn't leave a single thing out, I know I didn't! Who's going to buy a loaf looking like that?'

Her mother put her arm round her.

'Let's have a look at that recipe.' She picked it off the corner of the table where Henny had left it. 'Fruit ... sugar ... tea ... flour—that's it. It's not your fault, Henny, you did exactly what it tells you. But you used the flour out of the jar, didn't you?'

Henny nodded, still sobbing.

'That was plain flour. You need baking powder with it, you see, to make it rise. The egg on its own doesn't make it airy enough.'

'It certainly doesn't,' said Michael. He picked up the oblong piece and tapped it on the table. 'It sounds like a piece of wood. You could try selling them as doorstops.'

'Put it down, Michael,' said his mother, taking it from him and replacing it on the tray. Jack climbed on a chair and began surreptitiously to pick out the fruit.

'Why didn't she say so, then? I call that pretty stupid.'

'It didn't occur to her. She comes from the south, and she uses self-raising flour, and I'm from the north, and I use plain. Poor Henny, I *am* sorry.'

'But what am I going to *do* with them? No one's going to buy them like that, are they?'

'Well, it's no good crying over spoilt loaves,' Michael pointed out. 'We'll just have to think of something ingenious. I know! What about Guess the Weight? You'd really baffle people. They'd never guess. They'd be bound to say they're much lighter than they are.'

'Yes, but that wouldn't be any good.' Henny's sobs died down to the occasional sniffle as she began to get to grips with the problem. 'Guessers don't have to be *right*, the winner's the one that gets closest. And anyway the prize *is* the cake, and no winner is going to be pleased with one of those.'

'You could let people pick out the fruit, like Jack,' said Michael. He lifted him off the chair and put him on the floor, pushing the wire tray to the middle of the table. 'You could offer them ten raisins for a penny.'

'Or as many as they could pick out in five seconds! Say ...,' Henny's eyes began to light up, 'I wonder how many raisins there are altogether?'

Henny's mother gave her a slight push.

'I hope you can think of something, love. You go and work on it, and let me get myself something to eat. I'm perished. My feet nearly stuck solid while I was waiting for the bus. All the ponds were freezing over in the parks. Bad weather for birds at this time of the year.'

Henny stopped in her tracks.

'That's given me an idea ... At least, I think it has. I'll have to brood about it.'

'Tell us,' said Michael.

'Not yet. I will if it works.'

Henny was busy in her room for the next half hour, emerging at intervals to look for scissors, paper, coloured pencils, and a large plastic bag.

Michael, who was swearing at a vital piece of his model which had come unstuck, and Mrs Cary, who was washing the last of the ill-fated mixture out of Jack's hair, let her get on with it.

By the time it was her bedtime, Henny's good humour had returned.

'Thanks to Great Aunt Dorothy,' she announced, 'our Spring Fair will have something really unusual for people to buy. A truly unique and fascinating offer.'

'What exactly are you planning?'

'I won't tell you at the moment, just in case it's not a success. I'll tell you tomorrow.'

Mrs Cary turned the key in the front door with frozen fingers and some apprehension. How had the Spring Fair gone?

The kitchen door flew open and Henny shot out.

'Mum! Mum! It was a great success! Both my pin cushions went, and the girls' table beat the boys! And my idea helped to do it, because every bit of the fruit things sold! Sir said I showed enterprise and inge-ingew-in-ge-nuity.'

'Henny, I *am* pleased.' Mrs Cary stuffed her gloves in her coat pocket and followed her into the kitchen. 'So now you can let us into the secret! What *was* your bright idea?'

'I told the others already. Even Michael admitted it was great. Look!'

She picked up a large sheet of paper from the table and held it up.

'I worked it out last night and did it this morning at school. And don't tell me—I know some of the spelling's wrong. And I don't see that it mattered, because heaps of people read it, and almost everyone who did bought some. There! Isn't it eye-catching?'

At the top Mrs Cary read, in bright red letters:

DON'T LET YOUR
FETHERED FREINDS
FREEZE TO DEATH!

Underneath, in blue and green letters alternately, was:

When its icy cold (like today)
birds can't find food and they
can DIE.
Buy our speshal extra-rich
consentrated birdfood

—and then, in a final blaze of red—

AND HELP THEM LIVE!!!

At the end, in discreet black, were the words:

Only 5p a piece.

'See? And Sir helped me to cut it all up into chunks, and I wrapped each chunk in a piece of paper, and I explained to everyone how it was full of goodness and birds would love it and how they would enjoy seeing their feathered friends tucking in, and how it would only cost them five pence to do such a good deed and get such satisfaction. Heaps of people bought a piece, and Mrs Staples bought four, because she said she had a robin *and* a blackbird *and* lots of tits in her garden. And then the funniest thing! After all that, I won the raffle! For the very first time! The fifth prize! And you'll never guess what I got ...!'

'A basket of fruit? A doll? A box of chocolates?'

'Nothing like that! I'll show you.'

Henny climbed on to the blue kitchen chair which had been left near the sink, and tugged at the blind. It flew up with a clatter. On the far side of the window pane Mrs Cary could see a bright red spiral shape filled with pieces of bread and miscellaneous bits and pieces.

'It's a special bird-feeder. Mrs Staples is nutty on birds, and she got given two for Christmas, so she gave one to the Spring Fair, and I won it! It sticks on the window, Michael put it up, and you fill it with food. You're supposed to use peanuts and things like that, but we didn't have any, so I just put in the left-over scraps from the refreshments. Silly, isn't it? By the time they did the raffles I'd sold all my special bird stuff. I'll get some peanuts with my pocket money tomorrow, and we can put in bits of apple core and bacon rind and things like that, so it won't cost much. And even though we haven't got a garden, I'm sure the birds will find out where there's food, and you'll be able to watch them from right close by. You'll like that, won't you? But wasn't it a funny coincidence? Sir said it must be fate.'

Mrs Cary reached up and pulled down the blind.

'If it is, it's a nicer one than most. I wonder what birds we'll get first?'

'I bet they'll be queuing up in the morning,' said Henny confidently. 'Just you wait and see!'

6

The Midnight Visitor

Henny felt herself dragged awake, pulled from dark depths of sleep. She lay there, trying to make herself dive back again into the delicious warmth.

It was no use. She could hear the wind beating against the house, making its eerie whistling sounds down the boarded-up chimney.

Then she heard another sound, regular and persistent. She half pushed herself up in bed. There it was again. Very thin, high and piercing. She pulled the quilt up over her head, but she could still hear it. Sometimes it would stop for a few seconds, and Henny would start to relax, but then it would start again, each time harder to ignore.

She pressed her hands over her ears and squeezed her eyes tight shut, but the noise spiralled its way into her head.

A cat. But surely a very small cat. Perhaps just a kitten?

The wind blew louder, and tossed handfuls of rain and hail against the window. Henny pictured a small shivering creature.

'Damn, damn, damn!' she muttered, and sat up sharply.

There were rustling noises below.

'Henny?'

'Mmm.'

'Henny, I got woke up.'

'You're not the only one.'

'I'm *tired*, Henny. I've been awake for hours and hours and *hours*. I'm going to tell Mum.'

'Oh no you don't! You just lie there and keep quiet.'

Groaning, Henny pushed her toes out from under the quilt. She swung down from her bunk on to the edge of Jack's, and jumped on to the floor. The air was cold and shivery. A faint light filtered round the edges of the curtains but it was too dark for her to find her slippers. She decided against putting the light on and managed to grope around until she found her dressing-gown.

She stood in the dark hallway, listening. The piercing wail was fainter now. It seemed to come from the back of the house. There was no sound from the front room: her mother must be still asleep. A pale oblong of yellow light shone along the hall from the glass panel over the front door. She padded along towards the kitchen. She paused for a moment outside Michael's room. All was silent. Nothing ever woke him up once he'd got to sleep—he could even ignore the noisy alarm clock that lived on the biscuit tin by his bed.

She pushed open the kitchen door and switched on the light. The brightness hit her eyes, and the chill of the tiled floor nipped her feet. Curling up her toes and walking on the sides of her feet, she took the key off the hook and unlocked the back door.

She hesitated for a moment. The wail was much louder now. It seemed to come from just outside. But suppose it was a trick? Suppose it wasn't a cat, or a kitten. Suppose it was a someone, or a something, sounding like a kitten?

Very cautiously, she opened the door. With the light behind her, the outside looked very dark indeed.

The wail was much louder, and faster.

She opened the door wider.

In through the gap shot a thin wet ginger streak.

It thudded against Henny's legs, leaving cold wet patches, tore across to the cooker, hurtled back, spun off

towards the table, rushed back, and then wound round Henny's ankles. She shivered at the touch of damp fur. The wail was replaced by a high, frantic purr.

'There, there,' said Henny. 'You're all right now!'

The purrs redoubled, and Henny saw that it was bigger-than-a-kitten but still-smaller-than-a-cat. It had grubby white paws and a grubby white neck and dark blue eyes, and it was wet and very hungry.

'You'll soon be dry.'

Henny shut and locked the door. She couldn't possibly turn the poor thing out again—surely her Mum and Michael would see that.

She opened the fridge door and took out a bottle of milk. It was colder than the cat, colder even than her feet. She took a saucepan, carefully lit the stove, and poured a good stream of milk into the pan.

She took a bowl off the shelf, emptied the milk into it, and set it on the floor. The cat leapt towards it, sending it skittering across the floor. Then, as it caught up with it, the purring stopped dead. All Henny could hear was a steady, rhythmical lapping.

Henny looked down with satisfaction, but all her inner glow didn't prevent her from feeling suddenly very cold, very tired, and very keen to get back into bed. She looked round, wondering where the cat could sleep, and spotted an old grocery box under the table. She pulled it out, and lined it with old newspaper. She waited for the cat to finish, and then bent down, and picked up its light, bony body and placed it in the box. The cat gave a lively, startled purr, and leapt out again. Henny put it back. The cat jumped out. It purred, if possible, even more loudly than before.

'In you *go*,' said Henny firmly. She picked up the cat, held it over the box, and dropped it in. Racing to the kitchen door she nipped through and shut it. She heard a faint, exhausted mew, and the soft scuffle of a body against the door, then silence. She'd not turned off the light, but if the cat was anything like as tired as she now suddenly felt, nothing was going to keep it awake.

Yawning, she started back down the hall. Jack had fallen asleep again, and didn't stir when she climbed past him back into her bunk.

She felt for the sweater she had thrown on her bunk the night before, and wrapped it round her frozen toes. Before she had time to start worrying about what would happen next morning, she was asleep.

'Mum! Mum! There's a cat in the kitchen!'

Jack's voice woke Henny with a start.

The cat.

Yes.

Well.

Oh dear.

Henny shot out from under the quilt and jumped to the floor.

The cat looked larger, fluffier, and more brilliantly orange than the night before. It was also, if anything, louder. It flung itself on Henny as she came into the kitchen, and purred so hard its whole body shook like a clockwork train. Henny bent down and stroked it.

Footsteps padded along the hallway.

'However did that get in here?'

Henny's mother, her dressing-gown pulled hastily round her shoulders, gazed in disbelief.

'It's not a that, it's a cat,' protested Henny. 'Just a kitten, really. It's lost and there's no one to look after it.'

'Ah, the poor wee creature,' exclaimed Michael, picking up an imaginary violin which he started to play. 'Abandoned by all, and never a friend but Henny!'

'Shut up, Michael! If you didn't sleep like a log you'd have heard it too. I'm sure if you'd heard it you would have let it in, Mum. I only opened the door a crack and it shot in.'

'Well, now it can just shoot out.'

'Oh, it can't, Mum! It hasn't had any breakfast!'

'It can go and get breakfast at its own home.'

'Supposing it hasn't got a home? It was ever so hungry, truly. And it's still raining. You can't turn a poor little kitten out on a day like this!'

'As if I didn't have enough to think about, Henny! We are not going to keep a cat. I've told you before. It's not fair on any animal to be shut up all day—it isn't as if we had a garden. Now go and get dressed, the lot of you, or we're all going to be late.'

Henny looked at her mother's face and said no more. She waited until breakfast was over (the cat having been temporarily banished to the bathroom) to ask, 'Please, Mum, couldn't we give it just a bit to eat?'

Mrs Cary sighed resignedly.

'I suppose we'll have to. All right, Henny. Open a tin of sardines and mash up a couple with a bit of bread. We're not keeping it, though! It can stay today, but when you get back from school you can go round with Michael and see if you can find who owns it.'

'Have a heart, Mum!' protested Michael warmly. 'I won't have time to do that! It's maths *and* geography tonight, and I'm not missing television because I've spent hours and hours knocking on doors. Why don't we put a card in the shop on the corner? Everyone round here reads those. If Henny does one now, she can take it on her way to school.'

'All right. You'll find some brown envelopes on the mantelpiece in the front room Henny. Don't use any more than you can help. Work out the words on a piece of scrap paper first.'

Henny sat frowning at the kitchen table.

After much thought, she started:

Found, a ginger cat.

Then she began again, and put:

'Have you lost a ginger CAT?'

She crossed out 'CAT' and put 'KITTEN'.

Then she added 'or a small cat. With blue eyes.'

She stopped again, and studied the cat, which was contentedly licking itself on the doormat.

Then she took a deep breath, and made a fresh start.

'HAVE YOU LOST A SMALL GINGER CAT
or a fairly large Kitten
with blue eyes and BLACK whiskas
and 3 white paws and a WHITE neck
and a LOUD PURR.
If so please call at 63 Linden Road.'

After reading it through she added 'and 1 ginger paw' (for otherwise it sounded as though it was one leg short), and began to copy the words out on one of the brown envelopes. It was going to be a tight squeeze.

Her mother, putting on her earrings, stopped to read over her shoulder.

'That's fine, Henny, but don't put the address. Just the phone number.'

'What for, Mum? Lots of people haven't got phones.'

'If they've lost their cat they won't mind looking for a phone box. I don't want anyone turning up and discovering the house is empty. Here's ten pence for the card. Put some newspapers on the floor in case it makes a mess. Come *on*, we've got to go.'

Henny watched Mr Hall pin up the envelope in his small cabinet, making sure that he put it right in the middle where it could be easily read, and not at the top where passers-by would have to crane to see it.

She thought about the cat most of the day, and drew a picture of it in her Nature Topic, which was Wild Life in Danger.

When she got home she hovered by the telephone, but no grateful owner rang claiming a small cat (or large kitten), and though Henny didn't mind *very* much clearing up the mess it had left in the kitchen, she knew she would not look forward to doing it every day.

All was forgiven though when the cat, following supper (bought by Mrs Cary in her lunch hour) lay purring heavily on her lap.

'What *are* we going to do with you?' she said, tickling it under the chin. The cat lurched forward and nearly toppled off her knees. It closed its eyes and its small pink tongue stuck out. 'That's all very well, but Mum's right. You can't stay here. Our yard at the back's so small I couldn't swing you round even if I wanted to. It's even smaller than the sandpit in the nursery class ...'

'If we don't find where it's come from, Henny, you'll have to find somewhere else for it to go. Can't you ask around at school?'

'Let's wait a bit longer. They mightn't have seen the notice yet.'

'There's no harm in asking. After all, who knows how far it's come. If something frightened it, it could have run for miles.'

'Poor little scrap,' said Henny, tweaking its ears. 'Did something horrid scare you?'

The cat twisted over in her lap and lay with its four paws flapping like worn out pipe cleaners. It purred diligently, and seemed unconcerned. 'You ought to have a name. You can't go on being called It.'

'It's probably Ginger, or Marmalade, or Orlando.' Michael looked up, grateful for the interruption. 'I'd put my money on Ginger.'

'*I* think it should be Toffee,' said Henny. 'Pleased to meet you, Toffee—how do you like your name?'

Toffee rolled over and fell asleep.

No one rang the next day.

Or the next.

Or the day after.

Mrs Cary bought a tray, and cat litter, and cat scraps from the market. Toffee licked his plate twice a day, slept in Henny's lap all evening, and even remembered to use the tray occasionally.

But on Thursday night, when Mrs Cary came back to find an even more pungent smell than usual in the kitchen, she waited until they had all finished supper, and said, 'Look, Henny, we can't go on like this. It was a good notice you put in the shop, but it doesn't look as if Toffee's owner has seen it, does it? Have you asked at school whether anyone would like a cat? Well, don't forget, do it tomorrow will you?'

Henny shook her head sadly.

And next day she tried.

But Kim already had two cats.

Kevin's older sister had a dog.

Dennis said his mother didn't want a cat to fall over as well as Bridget and Deirdre.

Rhona said cats brought her mother out in a rash.

George said that in their family a cat would just get stood on, and Martin said his Nan had a canary.

Only Arabella, coming back with Henny on Friday night, offered a gleam of hope.

'Jessica's always said pets are just too complicated, but I don't suppose she's ever thought how elegant a cat could be. A handsome cat like Toffee would look stunning sitting in the window of DECOR. Besides, she's ever so soft-hearted. I'll mention it tonight. And I bet if we take Toffee down to the shop tomorrow morning, she'd agree in a flash.'

'I've an old grocery box I could put him in to carry him along. I don't suppose he'll like it, but I expect we can manage him between us,' said Henny.

Bella promised to turn up first thing next morning;

and when Mrs Cary came back—late, as she often was on Friday—from work, Henny told her that it looked as though their Toffee-problems might be over.

'Thank goodness! I had no luck at the office at all. Everyone who wants a cat's already got one, and all those who haven't don't want one. Let's just keep our fingers tightly crossed.'

Next morning, as Henny had feared, Toffee protested strongly at every attempt to imprison him. It was only when Michael got out of bed to come and help that they finally succeeded in getting the cardboard box shut and tied with string.

Toffee-in-a-box proved an awkward parcel to handle. As Henny and Bella set off down the road, carrying him between them, they could feel him lurching and sliding from side to side. His paws pushed out of the thin gaps between the cardboard, poking and twitching like furry tarantula legs, and he set up such a high-pitched wail that people they passed in the street turned to stare after them.

By the time they reached DECOR they were feeling very hot and bothered.

'I hope your Mum's glad to see us.'

'Well ... she's always glad to see you, Henny.'

'Bella!' Henny caught something from the note in her voice. 'You *did* tell her we'd be bringing Toffee?'

'Well, not *exactly*, Henny. I did say that I thought a cat would add that extra homely something to the shop—sort of make it more *genuine*, less *commercial*.'

'And what did she say to that?'

'She said, "Yes, darling, very likely." '

'But was she *listening*, Bella?'

Bella shrugged, jerking the box. Toffee yowled louder than ever.

'You *know* what Jessica's like. You can't really tell. I thought if I told her *definitely* that we were bringing

Toffee, she might pay attention and tell me not to.'

'After lugging him all this way, I just hope and pray that she takes to him.' Henny was beginning to feel that for two pins she could just put the box on the ground, let Toffee out, and wish him good luck and good riddance.

Fortunately, the very next road was Casson Street, and with Bella leading the way they edged their way cautiously through the glass door of DECOR.

Jessica was on her own, feeding a shining cascade of brilliant blue into her sewing machine. At the sound of Toffee's one-cat protest movement, she looked up and took her foot off the switch.

'Hello, Henny. Hello, darling, I wasn't expecting you back so soon. Whatever have you got in there? What a truly fearful racket.'

'It's only Toffee, Mrs—Jessica.'

'It's certainly the most talkative toffee I've ever come across.'

Henny smiled weakly.

Taking a deep breath, and looking accusingly at Arabella, who remained unusually silent, she undid the knot, the flaps of the box jumped upwards, and out popped Toffee's head.

As soon as he could see he was no longer trapped, he seemed quite content to stand there peering out of the box gazing inquisitvely around with his bright blue eyes. His fur shone, his white markings were snowy and his black whiskers fanned out in an aristocratic droop.

'What a handsome puss! But why have you brought him here?'

'I *told* you Jessica. He'll look ever so handsome by the fireplace, just the extra touch you need in the shop. See—like this!'

DECOR and ANTIQUES had been made out of the front rooms of two adjoining houses. In the side wall the old shiny black fireplace was still in position.

Bella lifted Toffee out of his box and placed him on the fluffy sheepskin rug in front of the brightly-polished brass kerb.

'There—you see? And in the depths of winter, when you have your little bit of fire, Toffee can sit and doze in front of it, and lots of people will come in the shop because it looks so cosy.'

'I like the way his fur matches the tiles,' Jessica said. Toffee stretched and sprawled and collapsed in a heap. 'He even goes with the mahogany mantelpiece. And as you say, he'd look even more harmonious in winter ... But we must be practical, darlings. He can't live here, can he? And however would I get him to and fro? No, Arabella, elegant though he is, I don't believe it's possible.'

Henny knew that more persuasion was needed.

'All you need is a cat basket, Jessica. You can get them in the market. I could save up and help to buy one. I'm sure he wouldn't be any trouble, once he'd got used to it. And he's such a nice cat'.

Anxiously, Henny walked over and squatted down next to him tickling him behind the ear. 'Come on,' she said to him under her breath, 'you do your bit. We've *got* to find a home for you somewhere.'

Toffee closed his eyes and stretched out his neck and his purr filled the room.

'He certainly looks at home! Maybe you're right ...' The doorbell rang and interrupted her. 'Hang on a minute, darlings, here comes Mrs Aleck for the sampler she asked me to repair. Good morning, Mrs Aleck, I have it here all ready for you, but I thought you'd like to see it before I wrapped it.'

'I think she'll take him,' whispered Henny.

'I do hope so. He's a darling—aren't you, Toffee?'

Toffee continued to purr. His chin dropped lower. He was almost asleep.

'About a new frame now, Mrs Aleck, I'm not sure if

we've one the right size. I'll pop next door and ask my husband, if you don't mind waiting a moment.'

Jessica Roach walked across the shop and through the door dividing DECOR from ANTIQUES, leaving it half-open behind her.

The DECOR bell ding-donged again.

In walked a short plump woman tugging a small shaggy dog on short shaggy legs on a bright red lead. It give a preliminary snuffle as it came through the door. Toffee stopped purring abruptly, opened his eyes, stiffened, and lay there twitching his tail in a meaningful way. The plump woman and the dog moved across the room. The dog's tail waved cheerfully as he looked around for something of interest.

He spied Toffee at the very moment Toffee rolled over on to his stiffened legs and perched there tensely like a stretched-out rubber band.

The dog began to yap with excitement. He jerked towards the fireplace. Toffee took off and dashed across the room, through the door into ANTIQUES.

Henny and Bella sprang to their feet and rushed after him.

They were too late.

There was a horrible clatter and the scrunch of breaking glass and the even more distressing sound of Mr Roach saying very unpleasant things in a very unpleasant voice.

Toffee tore back through the door and hurtled up the curtains by the window. The dog and the short plump woman tugged with equal energy at opposite ends of the lead. Henny, hot with worry and disappointment, rushed to the curtains. Toffee, just out of reach, clung and quivered.

Bella's parents shot through the door.

'Who the *** let that *** animal into my *** shop?—My apologies, Mrs Aleck. And you, Madam,' said Mr Roach, grinding his teeth. 'And what is it doing

clawing its way up Italian brocade at £14 a metre?'

He stalked across to the window.

Toffee tried to move higher, but the weight of his body had driven his claws into the material. He hung there powerless to move.

Mr Roach plucked him off.

'Don't hurt him, Mr Roach! He didn't mean any harm. He's frightened.'

Henny reached towards the cat.

Mr Roach looked for a moment as though he didn't know whether to hand him over or hurl him across the room, but then he put him into Henny's arms. Toffee scratched her across her hand, but she managed to grasp him and carry him over to his box. With great difficulty Bella and Henny crammed him into the box and folded the flaps across. Henny, her fingers fumbling with the knots, finally managed to tie up the string again.

'I'm very sorry, Mr Roach,' she apologised. There was a lump in her throat. 'I'm sorry if Toffee broke something. If you tell me how much it cost, I'll do my very best to save up and pay for it.'

'Humph!' said Mr Roach.

He went through the door and shut it loudly behind him.

Jessica put her hand on Henny's.

'There, darling, don't take on. Luckily it wasn't anything much. Just a rather boring pink glass candlestick. He'll have forgotten all about it by tonight. Still, darlings, it could have been something precious, couldn't it? I'm so sorry, Henny. But it really wouldn't do, would it?'

Henny shook her head. In spite of herself she was starting to cry. Everything seemed against Toffee.

'Don't fret about the silly candlestick, dear. I hope you find a nice home for the cat.'

Henny nodded without looking up. She picked up the

box. Toffee seemed to weigh even more than before.

'I'd better stop and clear things up,' whispered Bella, following her to the door. 'I'll call round later if I can.'

The shaggy dog was still barking as the door swung shut behind her.

'That's not Toffee back again?'

'Well, of course it is!' said Henny in exasperation, pushing past her mother as she opened the door. 'Empty boxes don't screech, do they?'

She pushed ahead of her mother down to the kitchen, and undid the box once again. Toffee staggered out with an expression of utter exhaustion, climbed on to the nearest chair, and promptly fell asleep.

Henny sat down on the next chair, leaned her elbows on the table, and plunged her head in her hands. Her mother walked over to the cooker, took off a pan lid, and stirred. Steam and a good smell filled the kitchen.

'Dinner won't be long,' said her mother comfortingly, 'and then we'll try and work out something. I hope Michael and Jack won't be too late. They've gone down to the market. Mr Marston called in and asked if someone could collect some vegetables for him. Mike said he was going anyway to get something for the animals in the lab.'

A sudden idea struck Henny.

'What about Mr Marston? He's on the ground floor and he's got quite a bit of garden, 'cause he's not on the corner like us. I'm sure he'd be good to Toffee.'

'I thought of that, Henny. I'm sorry, I don't want to be a wet blanket. But Mr Marston used to have a dog, and when it died he said no more animals, ever again. It was too hard to watch a pet die. He's often said so.'

Henny helped herself to a glass of orange squash and sat at the table, thinking. Her mother left the cooker and put up the ironing board. Toffee went on sleeping.

The telephone rang.

Her mother went through to the front room to answer it.

Henny heard the door shut behind her. Without giving herself a moment to change her mind, she picked up Toffee and put him in the box again. By now Toffee was too tired to protest. There was no scratching, and no wails. Even when she picked the box off the table he appeared to simply go on sleeping.

She walked down the hall, called, 'I'll be back in a minute, Mum,' and walked out through the front door before any questions could be asked.

Mr Marston looked surprised when he answered the bell.

'My goodness, that was quick! I wouldn't've believed Michael could have got there and back in the time. You got the things then, have you? Come along in, love, come right in.'

Henny followed him along the hall. It was just like theirs, but not like theirs. There were pictures of boxers wearing brightly-coloured clothes, and two rag rugs where they had plain red lino. The kitchen at the back had a blackened stove with a small fire glowing dimly inside it.

'That's very good of you, ducks. It's quite a walk for me to the market now, but I know you often go there weekends. Let me take that for you.'

He reached for the box. As he started to lift it from Henny's arms he tipped it up, and inside Toffee slid from side to side. There was a slippery scratching noise.

'Whatever ...?' exclaimed Mr Marston. He looked as though he might drop the box there and then.

Henny recaptured it, set it on the striped rug by the stove, and untied it. Toffee lazily pushed up his head, yawned, and sat there blinking.

'But that's not ...!'

'No. That's Toffee. I thought you'd like to meet him.'

In a rush, she began to tell the tale of Toffee's arrival about how she'd tried to find his owner; what a friendly, lovable, almost house-trained cat he was; how he'd nearly found a home that morning, and how they couldn't keep him because it wasn't fair on animals to be shut in all day, and that he'd make a marvellous companion for a kind and friendly owner.

Toffee, as though in agreement, jumped out of his box, gave himself a lick or two, yawned once more, lay down, and began to sleep again. A gleam of blue showed under his eyelids, and his pink mouth opened in a lazy purr.

'Don't you think it would be nice to come in and find him sleeping on your rug? He needn't cost much, either. We've got lots of bits like bones and fish skins and things like that. Truly, he hasn't cost us anything at all to feed, and he's a lovely friendly cat. I should think when a person's on their own they might sometimes be glad of a lovely friendly cat.'

There was a moment's silence.

Then Mr Marston said gently, 'Henny, there ain't nothing I'd like more than a lovely friendly cat. But when you get as old as me—well, you can't get used to people and pets dying. It makes you—it makes you very sad.'

Henny looked away from him, down at Toffee.

'I know, Mr Marston. Well, I mean I don't know but I can guess. Only ... well ... this is a very new cat, almost not a cat, more of a kitten still, and ... well ... some cats live for years and years. When my Mum was a little girl she had a cat called Mush that lived to be fifteen. So don't you think, since this is such a very very new cat ...' She paused, not knowing how to put it.

'It might last as long as me?'

Henny nodded, relieved that she hadn't had to say it.

Mr Marston laughed. A good, round laugh. He patted her head.

'I give you full marks for trying! Well, why not?' Awkwardly, he crouched down beside Toffee and gently stroked his back. The purrs redoubled, but Toffee's eyes shut firmly. 'Toffee and me, we'll keep each other company.'

Henny stood up.

'I'll let myself out,' she said.

Mr Marston tweaked Toffee's ear. He twitched it in irritation and curled around the other way. Mr Marston winked at Henny.

Yes.

They would keep each other good company.

7
Moving Day

It was Saturday. Lie-in day. Get-your-own breakfast and please-yourself day.

Henny pushed her arms out from under her quilt and stretched them above her head. The air trickled coolly over her fingers. She opened one eye and peered at the window. The white of the stripes in the curtain looked light and not grey. Good. That meant yesterday's rain had stopped.

Her arms were beginning to feel goosefleshy. She pulled them back into the warmth and shut her eyes again. It was one of her favourite times. Not quite asleep. Not quite awake.

Gradually she became aware of a drone from the bunk below her. Jack was awake and 'reading' one of his books.

'What is this animal pulling a cart. It is a horse of course. Where does it live? The horse-of-course lives in a stable.'

'Jack!' Henny opened her eyes. 'The word is *horse*, just *horse*.'

'The horse-of-course eats hay for breakfast.' Jack's voice rolled on. 'And the horse-of-course has hay for tea and hay for supper and carrots on Saturday. And of course the horse-of-course has sugar on Sundays.'

'Oh!' Henny bounced up in her bunk in irritation. 'I don't know why I bother. It's enough to drive a soul to breakfast.'

She reached down to the end of her bunk and

disentangled her dressing-gown from the sea of books, comics and socks banked up against the wall. She jumped with a crash to the floor and went to draw back the curtains. She pushed up the window and leant out. There were still puddles in the yard outside, but there were patches of blue in the sky.

The air smelt fresh and clean. Suddenly Henny wanted to be out of the house and away—off to the park, to the shops, to the market—anywhere as long as it was out. The next moment she remembered Dennis, slammed down the window and headed for the kitchen.

Michael was already there, wading through a large bowl of cereal and straining to listen to the weather forecast through the crackles of his small green transistor.

'Why don't you turn it up?' Henny asked, helping herself to a bowl and spoon. She took the half-empty bottle of milk from the draining-board.

'Because the batteries are going—can't you tell? Hey, what are you having Wheatflakes for? There's still a box of those Corncups left in the cupboard out of the three that you conned Mum into buying you so you could go into the competition. You ought to eat those.'

'I *am* eating them,' protested Henny. 'I have them every other day.'

'But you had Wheatflakes yesterday. I saw you.'

'Yes, today's my Corncups day, but I'm breaking my rule.' Henny spooned calmly away while Michael groaned and sank his head onto the table.

'You'll all be glad when I win! What are you going to do this morning?' she said, rapidly changing the subject.

'Going swimming with Vaughan and Ajaz, and no you can't come too.'

'I wouldn't have time anyway,' said Henny haughtily. 'I have plans of my own.'

'Oh?' said Mrs Cary, appearing in the doorway. 'What sort of plans?'

She moved over to the cooker and put on the kettle.

'Dennis is moving house today. I'm going to go over to help.'

'Won't you be in the way? Did they ask you to?'

'Not exactly,' said Henny diplomatically. 'But they're bound to be pleased if I do. There'll be lots of packing and such-like, and Dennis is a bit of a muddler.'

'And you're *not*?' said Michael incredulously. 'Do you know, Mum, she's got a whole piece of window sill in her class as well as her desk to keep her overflow on? I saw it when I went to the Open Day.'

'Shut up, Michael! Go on, Mum, it'll be all right.'

'Where are they moving to?'

'It's only the other side of the park, but it's going to be a proper house, a little one, but all their own, downstairs *and* upstairs. They won't have to share it with anyone like we do, and Dennis is going to have a room all to himself. Only a little one, though,' she added, seeing her mother pause as she reached for the bread, 'only a little room like Michael's. They need a house lots more than we do, 'cause he's got *four* brothers and sisters, so it's an awful squash where they are. And the people who live upstairs are *horrid*, not like the Nicholsons. They drink and swear and fight all the time.'

She watched her mother start to slice the bread, and then said, 'Can I go then, Mum? Can I?'

'All right, Henny. But don't get in the way. And make sure you're back by one.'

Henny dressed quickly, handicapped only briefly by a search for her shoes—which she had kicked off under the sofa or Mum's bed—and for her anorak, which she found in a corner of the bathroom.

As she went out of the front door the street felt full of Saturday. It was quite different from weekdays, much busier than Sundays: a bearded man carried a lawn-mower, a teenager had two bicycle tyres over one shoulder, people were cleaning cars, and old ladies with sticks and squashy felt hats were on their way to market.

It was a good day to be moving. Sunny, and dry, and full of bustle.

The first thing she saw when she turned into Sebastopol Grove was a large navy-blue van outside Dennis's house. The tail-lights were flashing as it squatted importantly across the road. The first thing she heard was a jangling piano playing the chorus of one of the hymns they'd learned for the last harvest festival. As she drew nearer to the van the music grew louder. 'Bread of heaven, bread of heaven, shall we ever give to thee ...' she hummed.

The music stopped, and started again.

She walked up to the van and looked into the dark depths beyond. A pale blob looked back at her. Squashed between a wardrobe and a kitchen cabinet was the Guigans' old piano, and squeezed in front of it was the performing Dennis.

'Hi, Dennis! What you doing there? Why aren't you inside helping?'

Dennis left the piano and edged past two chests of drawers.

'Ain't nothing left for me to do. There's a couple of blokes helping with the packing, shoving things in crates and that. Mum told me to hop off, said if the blokes dropped somefink she'd get compensation, but if *I* did all she'd get was the broken bits.'

'So there's nothing for me to do then either?' Henny felt disappointed.

Dennis shrugged.

'You can go and ask, if you like.' He jumped down. 'Come on, it's a madhouse in there.'

They were nearly bowled over by an approaching bed, but managed to scrape past into the back kitchen. Dennis's mother was standing watching his two younger sisters slowly downing glasses of orange squash, while from the front room came thumps and bumps and the heated voices of his father and two older brothers.

Mrs Guigan looked up as they came in.

'Oh, Henny, what a time to call!'

Henny felt wounded. Her Saturday lost its glow.

'I thought I could help.'

'Sorry, love!' Her voice softened. 'It's all taken care of. In a manner of speaking, anyway.' She leant forwards to mop up a dribble off Bridget's dress. 'Except—tell you what, how'd you and Dennis like to take this couple of beauties across the park to Acacia Road? There won't be any room for them in the car. Their auntie was going to take them for the day, but she's come down with 'flu. Fancy getting it this time of year! I'd never trust Dennis with the both of them, but if you was to go along as well, it'd save me the walk and I could do with the time.'

Dennis made a face, but Henny, looking at Deirdre and Bridget, reckoned that they seemed no worse than Jack and would at least have the charm of novelty. She nodded her head.

They were no worse than Jack. They were, on the other hand, no better. Bridget, who was older than Jack, never stopped talking and never looked where she was going. Deirdre, who was younger, hardly said a word, but knew exactly what she wanted to do, which was to swing on every swing, see-saw on every see-saw, and try to climb the large slide which said quite clearly CHILDREN OF SEVEN AND OVER ONLY.

'We'll be all day getting there at this rate,' said Henny, struggling to lift Deirdre, who was plump as well as determined, up to the drinking fountain.

'They're always like this,' said Dennis resignedly. 'A right pain in the neck. I never go out wiv 'em if I can 'elp it. Here, Dee, I'll give you a piggy-back.'

He squatted down so Deirdre could climb on his back. 'Come on, get on.' He gave a colossal yawn.

'I can see right down your froat!' said Bridget, gleefully.

'Shut up and start walking!'

'You feeling all right, Dennis?' Dennis always looked pale. He was one of the smallest boys in the class, with a thin face, dark eyes and dark hair. Today he looked even peakier than usual and, as her Mum would have said, the bags under his eyes looked as if they hadn't been unpacked for weeks.

'Yeah, I'm O.K. But we bin up for hours and hours, and me Mum and Dad and Terry was bangin' around 'alf the night. Didn't 'ardly get no sleep.'

'Let me have Dee for a while.'

'No, 'sall right. Well, O.K. Swop over when we get to the pond ... Thanks, Henny.'

With Deirdre out of mischief, and Bridget gripped firmly between them, they managed to get through the rest of the park and across the zebra crossing without any further delays. From there it was only five minutes before they reached the dark blue van now drawn up outside the Guigans' new house.

'There!' said Dennis with pride. 'That's a bit of all right, innit? Look, we got a front door, *an'* a back door, *an'* a side passage for the bins, *an'* a barfroom, and the landing's got a red rose in the window. Come on, I'll show you.'

Dodging past Mr Guigan and the van driver, who were coming down through the open door, they squeezed their way along the narrow hall to the back of the house. Mrs Guigan, imprisoned behind a stockade of teachests, was standing in a corner by the cooker.

'There you are then! I was wondering where you'd got to. Talk about a watched pot! I'll never get used to this electric. As for dinner, someone'll 'ave to go down to the takeaway. There'll be no cooking done in this kitchen today. Henny, be a love and take 'em all out in the back, will you?'

'Can't I help you in here? I could easily unpack some of these boxes.' Henny had seen more than enough of Deirdre and Bridget, and she liked unpacking things; it would feel like Christmas.

Mrs Guigan shook her head.

'No thanks, love. 'Tisn't something anyone else can do for me. I need to know where everything goes.'

'Can't I even show her the house first, Mum?'

'Not now, Dennis, 'ave an 'eart! You'd only be getting in everyone's way.' The kettle started to hiss. 'Tell you what though. You know that shed down the end? Well, it's all fallin' to pieces and your Dad's goin' to pull it down soon as he can. It's not safe with them two around. Full of rubbish, it is. You and Henny go down there and start sorting it out. I 'ad a quick look yesterday, and there's some things like plant pots and balls of string that's worth keeping. Dump the rubbish over by the wall so's your Dad can burn it later. And put anything worth 'anging on to just outside the shed.' She turned away to heat the teapot. 'Keep an eye on those kids and see they don't hurt theirselves, and don't none of you touch the broken glass in the window. I'll call you later to 'ave a cup of tea if there's any left in the pot. 'Ere, you can take these biscuits with you—no, *not* you Deirdre, Dennis'll share 'em out.'

She plumped a cosy on the pot, and climbed over the crates to unlock the back door. 'Now, don't you go damaging yourselves, mind.'

The back garden was little more than an outdoor

dustbin; piles of broken bricks, an old sink, blackened gas fires, bits of drain pipe, rotting floorboards, all knitted together with a tangle of weeds. Henny's eyes lit up.

'Cor, Dennis! What a great place! You might find anything here. You could find some really old coins under those bricks that'd been there for years and years, or a ring someone'd dropped, or ...'

'Or a pile of buried dog bones, more like. Come on, let's start on the shed. Here, Dee, Bridget, four biscuits each and mind you make them last. Remember what Mum said—you keep away from that broken window.'

Luckily, Deirdre and Bridget discovered a pool of water in the old sink, and began to amuse themselves pushing leaves across it with twigs. Then they hunted for daisies and dropped them in 'to make a lily pond'.

The shed door had lost a hinge and was leaning at an angle across the doorway. Henny and Dennis heaved at it to straighten it enough to make a gap for them to squeeze inside. Jagged patches of light fell through the broken window on the mess inside. What was left of the glass was so grimy and cobwebby that apart from these bright patterns the shed was shrouded in gloom.

'Pooh, it stinks!'

'There's been cats in 'ere.'

'Or rats.'

'Cor, Henny! D'you really think so?'

'I hope not. But last week George saw two rats at those broken-down houses at the end of his street. They were running in and out of the cellars.'

Together they stood at the doorway and peered into the shadows beyond. As their eyes got used to the darkness they could make out an old kitchen cabinet, an even older table, a bookcase with broken shelves, a stack of old deckchairs with torn material hanging from the warped frames, all buried under a jumble of seedboxes, petrol cans, lumpy plastic bags, old paint cans, and rotting cardboard boxes.

'This isn't getting us anywhere,' Henny pointed out. 'And your Mum wouldn't have sent us here if she'd thought there were rats.'

'She mightn't have known.'

'Then let's make sure.' She reached into a stack of bamboo sticks leaning by the door, and pulled out the longest. She began prodding into the heaps of rubble opposite. There were small rustles and mysterious rattles, and a clatter and a *bang* as an old saucepan without a handle tipped over and rolled from the top of a pile to the floor. But there were no squeaks. No eyes. Nothing scuttled across the floor.

'There, see?' Henny, becoming bolder, prodded harder and more wildly. 'There's nothing there. Just muck and mess. And plenty of that! Let's get it outside to start with. We can't see where we are in here. You get back outside, Dennis, and I'll pass you the stuff through the door.'

Once they got into the swing of it, Henny and Dennis found themselves getting carried away. Dennis staggered to and fro with boxes and bags and anonymous bits of old junk, while Henny pulled and dragged and heaved with increasing frenzy. She had almost got through to the bottom shelf of the bookcase when Dennis, puffing, said, 'Hey, Henny, that'll do! I'm worn out. I'm running out of space to dump stuff, anyway. We'd better start on the sorting.'

The sea of rubbish looked much too large ever to have squeezed into the small part of the shed which had been cleared. Deirdre and Bridget, much wetter and dirtier than when Henny had last seen them, were perched on two upside-down plant pots sorting through a box of damp and smelly comics.

She eyed the confusion with joy. It was much better than a jumble sale—and all free! Who knew what might turn up in one of those boxes? Who could tell what someone might have stored safely away and then forgotten about? But as she and Dennis began to work their way through the damp, dirty heap, her enthusiasm dwindled.

The pile of rubbish mounted rapidly. Old boots; ten-year-old newspapers; broken plant pots; corrugated paper; boxes of rags; painting sheets covered in mould; burnt saucepans; old paint cans with paint dried to broken cakes; torn plastic bags and a sack of cement set into a solid lump.

Over by the shed the small heap of things-worth-keeping grew very slowly indeed. A few plant pots; torn packets with seeds still left. ('They might come up, Dennis. It's worth a try'); a box of rusting tools ('We could have a go at cleaning them'); a twisted bird cage; old apple trays; a paraffin lamp; jam jars; a garden fork with a broken prong, and a box of dried-up bulbs.

'I'm fed up!' Dennis threw yet another broken pot on the rubbish pile. 'And I'm hungry. Didn't hardly get no breakfast. I'm going to ask me Mum when's dinner.'

'There's only three more boxes left.'

'You do them, then. Or shove them on the rubbish pile. They won't be worth looking at, I bet. You want to stay an' eat?'

'Mum's expecting me back. I'd better be going.'

'Stay 'ere just a couple of minutes with Dee and Bridget till I get back, will you?'

'All right. But mind you hurry.'

Henny reached for one more box as Dennis picked his way down the garden to the kitchen door. More rags, tin lids, and five rusting steak and kidney basins.

She reached over and pulled the last two boxes towards her; two wooden apple trays one on top of the other. The top one had odds and ends of string, and old lolly sticks with faded plant names written on them: 'CABBAGES' and 'CARROTS' and 'ONIONS'. She lifted off the top tray and poked around in the one

I DOZEN
LARGE

underneath. More string, torn bags of rusting screws, more sticks and labels and skewers.

Nothing exciting here, Henny thought as she ran her fingers through the muddle of bits and pieces. Then her fingertips touched something smoother amongst the rough screws.

From the bottom she pulled a small grimy stick. It was as thick as a pencil and almost as long as her hand.

She rubbed it. Loose grime and soil fell off. She spat on it and wiped it on her jeans. It was round and dark yellowy coloured, with rings cut into it at top and bottom and curling patterns down the side. She stirred around in the box some more and found another. And another. All of them were dirty, and most had soil clinging to the ends. In the end she found seventeen of them, each one different from the others.

She was binding them with a piece of thin green string when she heard the back door slam. Dennis clambered over the piles of bricks towards her.

'Look, Dennis. What d'you think these are?'

'You can see that. They're sticks, ain't they? Dad's just come back from the takeaway, and Mum says to bring Dee and Bridget back inside.'

'But they must be special sticks for something. Look at the patterns.'

'Yes, well, I dunno. I'm *starving*. Dad's got some crispy pancake rolls, and there's one for you.'

'Oooh, great! Dennis, d'you think your Mum'd mind if I took these? Just to find out about them?'

Dennis pulled the comics away from under Deirdre and Bridget. 'Couldn't say. Ask me Mum. Come on, inside you two! Don't suppose she'll be bothered.'

Mrs Guigan, pulling knives and forks from a half-unpacked crate, hardly looked up as Henny made her request.

'Go ahead, love! You take 'em if you want, and thanks ever so for helping Dennis, and keeping Dee and

Bridget from under my feet. You three go and wash, you can't eat nothing with hands like that, and Henny, you come back when we're a bit straighter, mind, and Dennis'll show you all over.'

Henny, going home with the bag with the pancake roll in one hand, and the bundle of sticks in the other, felt her morning had matched up to its promise after all.

Mrs Cary was not the sort of mother to fret over a little dirt, but even she winced when she saw Henny, her jeans smeared with dirt and grease, and with a further generous spattering of grime and cobwebs over hands, face and T-shirt. It was not until Henny had emerged from the bathroom that she consented to look at her small bundle of sticks.

'Well, now, fancy finding those! I wonder what they are? No, Jack you can't play with them now, it's time to eat.' As they sat down to shepherd's pie and carrots, Mrs Cary undid the string and let the sticks roll with a clatter on the table. 'I'm sure I've seen something like these before ... No, it's no good, I can't remember where. I like the different patterns. Why not take them down to the Roaches this afternoon? I expect they'll know about them.'

Henny found Arabella curled up on her favourite rocking chair in a corner of ANTIQUES, turning the pages of a large album of pressed flowers. She bounced up as Henny came in. The chair swung back, hitting the curved edge of a large gong standing on the floor just behind. Mr Roach sprang up from his desk, and Jessica opened the door between the two shops to see what was going on.

'Yes, certainly I know what those are!' she said, as Henny spilled the sticks on Mr Roach's desk. 'They're lacemakers' bobbins, aren't they, Douglas? Nice ones, too. You know, Henny, if you make lace by hand you have a whole lot of threads on different bobbins. The fancier the pattern, the more bobbins you need. Once, in Bruges, in Belgium, I saw a lacemaker using 140 bobbins at the same time! Her fingers flicked in and out so fast I couldn't see what she was doing. You found them in a shed? Well fancy that. These are quite old, you know.'

'Are they worth lots and lots of money?' asked Henny.

'It depends. Some people collect them. A few pounds, anyway. Yes, quite a few pounds. Do you want us to sell them?'

Henny explained how they weren't really hers, but Mrs Guigan's.

'She'll be excited, won't she?' said Bella. 'Let's go and tell her. It isn't every day you find something like that in a pile of rubbish.'

And indeed, when they went round to the Guigans', to find the whole family squeezed into the kitchen round yet more cups of tea, Mrs Guigan was full of *Well-I-never* and *Who'd-have-thought-it*, and when Henny told her what Mrs Roach had said, and asked her if she wanted to sell them, she said, 'A few quid'd certainly come in handy at the moment, that they would. Tell you what, Henny, you choose one of them to keep for your very own. And if Mrs Roach takes them into her shop and manages to sell the others, we'll give you a share as your commission like. If you 'adn't spotted them, chances are no one else would've. That suit you?'

Henny, beaming, said it did.

Weeks later Mrs Guigan came round with £3.50 for her in a brown envelope, and Henny put it into the Post Office to spend during the summer holidays. But part of her was even more pleased to know that sitting in a paste jar on her treasure shelf, beside her sea shells and two pearl buttons and the tiny bunch of flowers from the raffle doll and a green china duck from the market, there was a lace bobbin which might have been used by someone's great (or even great-great-great) grandmother, which she had rescued from the rubbish bin.

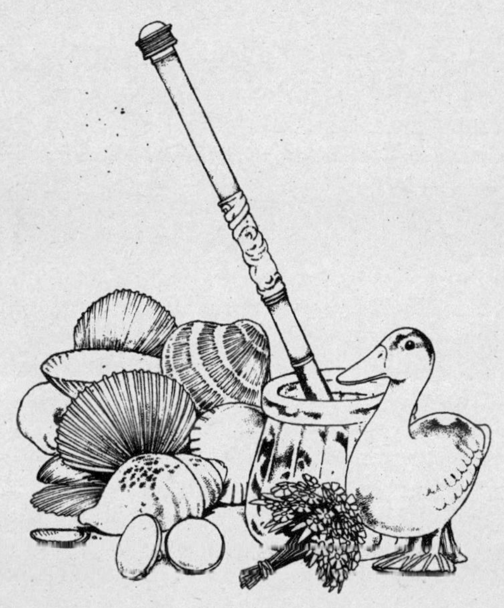

8

The Lost and Found Dog

There was no one at the bus stop. A bad sign. They'd probably just missed one, and that could mean a long wait. Bother Jack! If she'd been on her own she could have walked, but Jack took hours and hours.

'See, Jack?' she said crossly. 'If you hadn't gone back to get your gun, I expect we'd have been halfway to the market by now.'

'Bang! Bang!' Jack paid no attention. 'Bang!' He shot the man yawning in the door of the ironmonger's opposite, a small woman pushing a pram loaded with large bags of washing, and old Mrs Jenkins from number 36. Henny sighed loudly.

A dog trotting busily past paused at the sound, and stood beside them looking up enquiringly. Henny, who years before had once been bitten by Muffin, the yappy little terrier down the road, looked back at him with a certain caution. He was a middle-sized oblong dog, with a squarish head and long tail, covered with a mass of creamy hair, yellowing at the edges.

'Hello, dog,' she said.

'Bang! Bang!' Jack fired the gun at him with one hand, while with the other he slapped him hard on his wiry back.

The dog's curly tail wagged energetically.

'Nice dog! Good dog! *Great* dog!' The dog's long pink tongue flopped out of his mouth and he panted vigorously. 'Hey, Henny, I wish we had a dog.'

'You know we can't. Mum's boss would never let

her take a dog to work. And you couldn't leave a dog shut up alone in the house all day, could you?' Still, thought Henny, it was a pity. She would have loved a dog of her own. She would spend hours training it, so that it would obey her every word. It would lie across her door, guarding her at night; it would growl warningly at Steve, or Bernard, or Clive whenever she happened to meet them; it would field the balls in French cricket in the park.

The dog butted his head against her stomach—friendly, not frightening. She let him smell her hand, and rubbed his rough head. He leaned his warm weight against her.

'Sit then, dog! Good dog, sit!'

The dog, to her surprise, sat.

'See, Jack? He understands. I bet I'd be a really good dog-trainer, if I got the chance.' The dog licked her hand. His dark eyes looked at her trustingly. She bent down and put both her arms round his neck.

Jack moved closer to the dog's side, waving at him with his gun. 'Bet I could train dogs too. Bet I could be a *lion*-tamer! Hey, dog, stand!'

The dog wriggled impatiently in Henny's arms, and got to his feet.

'I told you so! He'll do anything I say. Here, dog, fetch!'

Jack raised his arm and was on the point of throwing his gun in the road when Henny grabbed him.

'Do you want to get him run over? Not to mention smashing your gun!'

Jack looked mutinous. For a moment Henny thought she might have a scene on her hands. But to her great relief she saw the bus rounding the corner. She grabbed Jack's hand.

'You wait till the bus stops, and then you get straight on. No fooling around.'

She put out a hand to stop the bus. It came to a neat halt with the door right in front of her.

She half-pulled, half-pushed Jack onto the platform, and spotting an empty seat halfway down the bus, made her way towards it.

'Wait a minute, love, not 'ere. Upstairs.'

The conductor, a small, tired-looking man with grey hair sticking out from under his cap, shouted from the far end of the bus, where he stood ready to pull the bell wire.

Henny stopped, startled.

'What for? There's seats down here.'

'I can't start this bus till you're upstairs. Be a good girl and get a move on.' The conductor's voice was louder than before. Passengers were starting to turn round. Henny felt uncomfortable.

'I can't go upstairs. Not when I've got Jack. Why should I?'

'Because dogs go upstairs.' The conductor sounded really cross now, and took his hand off the bell. 'No dogs downstairs, that's the rule. Either you takes your dog upstairs, or you gets off.'

'*Dog?*' Suspicion gradually dawned. Henny turned round to see the dog grinning cheerfully behind her on the platform. Pleased to be noticed once more, the dog started to move towards them.

'That's not our dog!'

'Come on wiv you, didn't it? And till it goes up or gets off, this bus ain't going to move.'

A large woman beside her looked irritably at her watch. Henny felt herself going pink.

'He's nothing to do with me!' Henny said. She pushed past Jack and leant down by the dog, pulling his collar round. A brass disc emerged from the long feathery fur under the chin. '20 Seaton Crescent,' she read. 'There you are! That shows you!'

'What d'you mean, it shows me? I dunno where you live, and I don't care, neither,' said the conductor hastily, seeing Henny open her mouth. 'All I know is, I want that dog *up* or *off*.' He moved back along the narrow corridor, pushing past Jack and Henny. '*Up*, or *off*!'

He bent forward and glared at the dog. The dog stood firm, drawing back his lips, growling gently, but pointedly. Somehow, Henny noted, the dog's face seemed to have lost its cheerful air. It looked distinctly cross.

The conductor seemed to share her feelings. He drew back sharply.

'People what own dogs oughter train 'em proper,' he announced to the bus at large. 'Nasty tempered creatures, some of 'em.'

Jack, who had been watching with quiet enjoyment, sprang to life.

'He's a *nice* dog! And he does what *I* say. You watch!'

Before Henny could stop him Jack had ducked under her arm and jumped off the bus.

'Come on, boy! Come on, good dog!'

The dog bounced after him, and Henny followed the dog, knowing that Jack would find it difficult to get back up again on his own. The conductor seized his moment. The bell rang.

Henny looked up to see the bus moving slowly away.

'Jack! *Now* look what you've done! There won't be another bus for ages. We'll have to walk.'

The dog sat down, whisking his tail to and fro across the pavement.

'Oh, well!' she said, making the most of it. 'At least it saves the fare. If we walk, we can spend the fares on something else.'

'Dog biscuits?'

'Certainly *not*! I expect he gets biscuits at home. Let's get going.'

Henny took Jack's hand and began to walk down the road. The dog got off its haunches and followed close behind. Jack noticed and pointed, laughing. Henny turned round. The dog sat down.

'Stay!' said Henny, unconvincingly. 'Go home!'

The dog flattened its ears and panted hopefully.

'Go home!' repeated Henny. 'If you come with us, you'll get lost.'

The dog crumpled into a heap, sagging sadly over its forepaws.

'Good dog!' said Henny. 'Stay!' She looked at him sternly. The dog's ears drooped. He dropped his muzzle onto his paws. 'Good dog!' said Henny again.

'Goodbye!' said Jack.

The dog said nothing.

Henny and Jack set off again.

'Don't turn round, Jack. If he sees we're not interested, he'll go home. Come on! Don't look.'

They walked silently along together, past the furniture shop and the wool shop and the West Indian and Continental grocery. No wet nose pressed in their hands. No wiry body flicked at their legs.

Henny and Jack, absorbed in wondering what was—or was not—going on behind them, failed to notice Kim and Arabella coming towards them.

'You've got a dog!' said Bella. 'I thought you couldn't have pets?'

'Does he bite?' asked Kim. 'What you call him?'

Resignedly, Henny turned to look. The dog bounced forward, and stood there, beaming.

'He hasn't bitten anyone *yet*,' said Henny. 'And we don't call him anything.'

'He's not ours,' said Jack. 'He's a friend.'

'I don't know about *that*,' said Henny. She was beginning to have doubts about a career as an animal trainer. 'We can't get rid of him.'

'Do you know where he comes from?' said Bella.

'20 Seaton Crescent.'

'Why don't you take him back, then?'

'You might get a reward,' added Kim.

'And bring joy to the heart of some poor child mourning its lost pet,' said Bella lyrically.

'I don't see as 'ow you've any choice,' pointed out Kim. 'You're stuck wiv 'im anyway.'

'I suppose I could go along to the market later,' agreed Henny. 'Or maybe Michael'll go ... All right then.'

'We'll come with you.'

'We'll all help.'

There followed a brief discussion over the whereabouts of Seaton Crescent, settled by asking a passing traffic warden, and the four of them set off.

The dog, apparently relieved that its future had been settled, got to its feet and trotted along behind them.

For the next five minutes all went well. The dog stopped when they did, crossed when they did, waited at traffic lights, and made no attempt to bark at bicycles or cars. Jack was delighted. He walked along with a hand on the dog's collar, grinning proudly at passers-by.

It was not until they approached the handyman's that Henny suddenly remembered what lay ahead. She grabbed the dog's collar.

She was too late!

The dog leapt forward. The two white cats that sat sunning themselves in the wire baskets of bargain offers outside hissed and spat and ran for safety. The dog followed. Tins and paint cans rolled clattering in all directions.

The handyman burst out of his shop, shaking his fist.

'You little ruffians! I'll get the police on to you. Just look at the mess!'

Henny and Kim and Bella and Jack hurled the tins at random back into the baskets before taking to their heels.

'Anyway, it's got rid of the dog,' said Henny philosophically.

'It hasn't,' said Jack. 'He's hiding behind the newspaper stand.'

He was right. A minute later the dog sidled up to them.

'I'm not taking him one step further!' said Henny. 'Heaven knows what he might do next.'

'All he needs is a lead,' said Bella.

'Or a piece of string,' said Kim. 'If we go round my place me Mum'll give us some.'

'We're more than halfway,' said Bella. 'We can't give up now.'

'I would if I could,' said Henny. 'But it doesn't look as if I can. All right then.'

They reached Kim's shop (Chas. Macgregor GREENGROCER Fresh Fruits and Salads Daily) without any further incident; the dog appeared subdued.

'Always room for one more,' said Kim confidently. 'Come on in.'

They all trooped in past the potatoes, cabbages, marrows, and the waiting customers to the kitchen at the back. Mr and Mrs Macgregor were too busy with their Saturday rush to do more than nod at them as they went through. Henny could never imagine what would happen if the whole Macgregor family tried to crowd in at once. Kim had three elder brothers and a sister and apart from Kim they were all very large.

The dog graciously accepted ginger biscuits and a bowl of water while Kim hunted for string; and seemed not to notice when she tied a length firmly to his collar.

'It's not very strong,' said Henny doubtfully.

'But he's not very big,' pointed out Bella.

'And we ain't got far to go,' added Kim.

'*I* want to hold him,' said Jack.

'Sorry, Jack. You're not strong enough. Tell you what, put your hand under mine,' said Henny.

'And we'll all take turns,' added Bella.

The dog patrol set off again.

Perhaps the dog was tired, or full of ginger biscuits, or simply determined to be on his best behaviour, but he trotted beside them as if no temptation known to dogs would be enough to make him forget himself. He was so perfectly behaved that even Jack was allowed to hold him on his own; and when they entered the park, they were beginning to congratulate themselves on a successful mission.

'There's nothing to training dogs, really, is there?' said Arabella.

'You just have to be firm,' said Henny, who was holding him at the time.

'And kind,' said Kim, bending down to pat him. 'Nice dog. How d'you like your walkies?'

The dog beamed, wagged his tail, and began to put on a turn of speed.

'Look at that. He knows he's going home!' said Kim, fondly.

The dog walked faster. He tried to break into a run.

'Hey! Stop tugging!'

The string began to cut into Henny's hand. She wrapped it round a couple of times and jerked the dog back. He started to pull again. The collar pressed against his throat. He made choking nioses.

'Henny, you're strangling him!'

'It's his own fault. I can't let him go here. You know what the keepers are like. Come *back*, dog!'

At that moment three ducks swooped over the ornamental pool and touched down on the top of the grassy bank which edged it. The dog lurched forward, the string snapped, and he threw himself wildly at the pigeons, ducks and moorhens which were idly dozing or paddling the afternoon away.

The next instant the air was loud with squawks and quacks as cursing birds took off in all directions, while others hurled themselves into the water. On the far side of the pool a keeper could be seen waving his arms and shouting in fury as he started to run towards them.

'Pack of hooligans!' he yelled. 'Dogs allowed only under proper control! Can't you read? Just you wait!'

'Not likely!' said Henny. She and Bella each grabbed one of Jack's arms, yanked him off the ground, and raced round the other side of the pond, with him dangling between them, towards the exit on the far side, while Kim tore ahead to make sure the gate was open.

The keeper rounded the pond and took a swipe at the dog, which ran off through the shrubbery to the gate. 'Don't you ever let me catch you with 'im 'ere again!'

'Don't worry, you won't!' said Henny in a heartfelt voice, but not so loudly that he could hear. 'Dogs simply aren't worth the trouble. Give me goldfish any day.'

'Don't look now, but 'ere 'e comes again!' said Kim.

Chastened by his encounter with authority, the dog pressed himself against the ground in an abject heap.

'I can't stand it!' said Henny. 'When I think of the peaceful afternoon we were going to have until that *monster* came into my life ...'

'Look,' said Arabella reasonably. 'Let's just walk on towards his house. It's only down the road there. If he comes with us, fine, we'll ring the bell and hand him over, and if he doesn't, great, we'll forget all about him and turn round and go back.'

'But not through the park,' added Kim.

'Certainly *not* through the park,' agreed Henny and Bella together.

They crossed the road and walked down the street on the opposite side. From time to time they glanced back. The dog continued to trot close behind, with a well-bred, butter-wouldn't-melt-in-its-mouth expression. Their spirits began to rise.

'Cor, these aren't 'alf posh houses!' said Kim.

'I bet whoever lives at number twenty is about to be

overcome with relief and gratitude,' said Bella. 'I bet they're about to reward us with a sign of their appreciation.'

They passed wrought-iron gates, neat brick paths, urns full of marigolds, gleaming windows through which they could see displays of luxuriant pot plants, small statues and huge pictures.

'My!' said Kim.

'Worth a pretty penny,' said Bella, appraisingly.

'Let's hope they're in,' said Henny.

Number twenty was one of the smaller houses, only two storeys tall, but every bit as prosperous-looking. There were metal grilles over the bottom windows and a burglar alarm over the front door. The brass door-knocker and letterbox twinkled away as though someone had nothing else to do all day but keep them clean and polished.

The dog pushed past them and sat on the doorstep.

'Here goes!' said Henny. She pushed the bell.

The dog pressed against the door and whined pathetically.

There was silence.

'You ain't ringing loud enough,' said Kim.

She leant heavily on the bell. A shadow appeared on the frosted glass panels. Very cautiously, the door opened, and a lined, heavily made-up face with very blue white hair peered out.

The dog whimpered. The face looked down.

'Oh, my precious little Pootsie-Wootsie!' it exclaimed.

'We've brought him back to you,' said Henny.

'We knew you'd be missing him,' added Bella.

The door opened a little wider.

'Did my little Pootsie-Wootsie miss his Mumsy-Wumsy then?' The dog pushed through without so much as a last tail-wag; they could hear his nails sliding across the polished floor inside. 'And as for you, you naughty little children, you ought to be ashamed of yourselves, taking a dear little doggie away from his home. You ought to be spanked, the lot of you. Be off with you, and don't let me set eyes on you again!'

The face vanished and the door slammed shut.

The four of them stood there, open-mouthed.

'The old witch!' said Kim.

'Did you ever!' gasped Bella.

Something cracked in Henny.

Leaning down, she pushed open the shining letterbox and shouted: 'We didn't take your rotten old dog! Your rotten old dog found us! He stopped us going on the bus, and he got us into trouble at the shops, and he chased the ducks in the park! We wouldn't want your rotten old dog if you paid us!'

She was shouting so loudly that she didn't hear the footsteps returning to the door. As a shadow fell again on the glass she stood up sharply, and the four of them started to run for the gate.

'Just a minute!' It was a man's voice. They turned round. This time the door was fully open. The man standing there was tall and thin and bald, with a very white shirt and a silk scarf round his neck. 'I heard what you said. Won't you tell me what happened?'

They told him. All four of them. In detail.

He held up his hand.

'I must apologise on Pootsie's behalf. I'm afraid he's caused you a lot of trouble.' He put his hand in his pocket and pushed a couple of notes in Henny's hand. 'Someone must have left the gate open this morning. I'm most grateful to you. Something dreadful could have happened to him if he hadn't met you, and we would have been most upset.' Lowering his voice, he said, 'Don't worry about what my wife said. She gets very worried about Pootsie. Thank you for your help.'

He watched and waited as the four of them turned back towards the gate.

'Goodbye!' he said, and gently shut the door. They closed the gate. Behind the gauzy curtain across the central upstairs window they could see a shadow.

'Ooh, she's a proper caution, she is!' said Kim.

'I pity her poor husband,' said Bella.

'She reminds me of a lady living near my Gran,' said Henny. 'Do you remember, Jack?' They started to walk round the park towards home. 'She's got a lovely house, and a huge garden, and round the edge where it meets the road it's got a row of white-painted stones. If you tread one *step* on to the grass she opens her window and shouts at you. And if you ever dare *stand* on one of the stones, like Jack did, she takes off her shoes and throws them at you.'

'She never!' gasped Kim.

'She does, you know. And she swears something terrible.'

'What does she say?' asked Bella.

'I couldn't *possibly* repeat it,' said Henny primly. 'Not in front of Jack.'

9

The Great Last Chance Family Holiday Competition

'Whew!' Henny took a long drink at the fountain, and then moved her head so the cool jet sprayed over her face and neck.

Shaking her head, she sent a spray of drops sparkling for a moment in the brilliant sun.

'I needed that! I thought I'd die of thirst inside. I feel like a tomato plant in a greenhouse. Even when Sir opens all the windows it's still too hot. If it goes on like this you'll see me putting out shoots.'

'I like it,' said Kim. 'I like not havin' to wear no socks and not havin' no cardigans to lose. Me Mum and Dad hate it though. All the spinach goes yellow and the lettuces go limp and the strawberries turn rotten soon as look at you.'

'Oh, I *like* it all right, only I'd like it a whole lot more if it wasn't school time. I don't feel one little bit like work.'

'Who does? Even Sir's getting crotchety. I bet he can't wait for the holidays. I'll be in the shop for the first couple of weeks, then I'm stayin' with me Nan, then the last fortnight me Dad's going to shut up shop and we're all stayin' in a caravan in Wales. Right by the beach. Somewhere called Abersomefink. What're you going to do?'

Henny squatted down in the nearest patch of shadow and leant back against a large concrete tub filled with dried-up marigolds.

'I don't know yet. Mum's got to stop work when

we're all at home, 'cos someone's got to keep an eye on Jack, and it's not easy when there isn't the money coming in every week. Last year we were lucky; we spent one week with one Gran and one with another and then two weeks with my Mum in a funny little place. You remember, the one I told you about, where Jack slept in a sort of cupboard and there wasn't a proper toilet and the pigs woke us up in the morning. That was fun. Michael went on and on about the pigs smelling awful, but I used to get up early and go and help the farmer with them. I like pigs. I wish we could keep one in the back yard but there wouldn't be room for it to turn round when it got really big. It'd have to stay facing one way all the time, and think how boring that would be, unless I could train it to do somersaults.'

'Don't be daft, it'd still end up the same way.'

'Not if I got it to stop halfway.'

'Then it'd be stuck on its back.'

'I'd have to teach it to twist over and land back on its feet. Still, I don't expect it would like it.'

'I don't suppose your Mum would either!'

'Michael *certainly* wouldn't, that's for sure.'

'There's the bell.'

Henny groaned, and struggled to her feet.

'Back to the prison cell. Roll on the holidays!'

'Mum, where *are* we going in the holidays?'

'Henny, what a time to ask! I've absolutely no idea just now.' Mrs Cary, pulling a lettuce apart in the sink, reached up a hand to push back the tendrils of dark hair sticking to her forehead. Even with both doors and window open, the kitchen was hot and sticky.

'Well, when *might* you have an idea?'

'At the moment, I truly couldn't say.' Mrs Cary turned on the cold tap and reached for the colander.

'Well, I wish you could. It's so hot and Jack keeps me awake all night saying how he can't sleep, and I get roasted alive in the classroom, and I want to go *away*.'

'Henny, it's no good going on like that. You know your Granny Lindsay's been ill. I hope she'll get better soon but I can't *know* if she'll be well enough to have you all, and I'm sorry I forgot to tell you, but your other Gran's going to spend the summer with her sister in Canada.'

'It's not fair!' Henny knew she was being unreasonable, but she could feel her dress sticking to her, she had a headache, and on the way back from school Bella had told her she was going to Italy. 'Other people go away! Why can't we?'

'Henny, use your head! Because we don't have the money, that's why. If Granny Lindsay's well enough to have you for a bit, then I can keep working, and I expect we can manage to get away somewhere. But if not—well, we'll just have to wait and see.'

She began slicing a short fat cucumber. The smell—a smell Henny usually loved—tickled her nose, but tonight she was too disappointed to notice it.

'Do you mean we might be here right through the summer? Never go away at all? Shut up here every day?'

'Yes, I do mean just that!' Mrs Cary's patience snapped. 'For heaven's sake, Henny, use your common sense! If we can't afford to go anywhere, then we can't afford to, and that's all there is to it. Now don't keep on at me, there's no point. Go and see what Michael and Jack are up to and keep out of my hair until supper's ready.'

Henny stalked out, furious but silent. She found Michael rearranging his collection of ship pictures while Jack sat on his bed and offered suggestions.

Since Michael's room was squeezed into the side of the house, and faced the dividing wall, it was cooler than the kitchen, but even so Jack's face was pink and damp, and Michael had taken off his shoes and socks and thrown his shirt on the bed.

Henny leaned against the doorway, glowering.

Michael hung up one picture, stood back to look at it, then turned and reached again for the hammer.

'What's up with you then? Lost a pound and found a penny?'

He began hammering at the wall again.

'I just asked where we were going in the holidays, and Mum flew off the handle.'

'Why didn't you wait until she'd had something to eat, you cuckoo? You know she always comes in tired.'

'I don't see it would've made any difference. She says we aren't going away anywhere this year. Nowhere at all. Probably not, anyway. She says we'll have to wait and see.'

Michael shrugged.

'Then we'll have to, won't we? I don't see why you're getting so steamed up.'

Henny suddenly remembered.

'It's all very well for you!' she attacked. 'You're going to scout camp for a fortnight. It was fixed weeks ago, and Mum's paid for it already. No wonder you don't care about me, or Jack,' she added piously.

'Don't be a pig, Henny. Even if I didn't go there wouldn't be enough to take us all anywhere. *And* I earned a lot of the money myself in the Christmas holidays, helping to clean out Mr Benedict's cellars. That wasn't much fun, I can tell you. In fact, I was just about as frozen then as I'm baking now.'

'Still, you *are* going away, and I *am* staying here, cooped up for weeks and weeks and there'll be no one to play with 'cos everyone *else* will be away too.'

'Shut up, Henny! Don't you think Mum'd like to get away too? And Jack? It's no good kicking up a fuss. Going around upsetting everyone's just daft. Addle-pated,' he added for good measure.

'Addle-pated,' repeated Jack happily. 'Daft, daft, daft.'

'I'd like to addle-pate *you*,' snapped Henny, going

out and slamming the door behind here. She retreated on to her bunk.

Up near the ceiling it was stuffier than ever. Henny lay there listening to Michael's tap-tap-tapping on the wall, and the intermittent rumbling in the pipes which meant that her mother was turning the tap on and off in the kitchen, and grumbled to herself. But she knew very well that what Michael and her Mum had said was true; if there wasn't the money to go away, there wasn't, and it was no good wishing for it.

'... so it looks as though we won't be going *anywhere*.'

Kim offered Henny a bite of the peach she'd brought to school.

'Well, heaps of people never ever 'ave a 'oliday,' she said philosophically. 'Tracy's never been more than a mile away from 'ere in any direction in all 'er life. Except when she was born, of course, 'cause that was in the 'ospital. 'Er Mum gets travel sick. Cars, trains, buses, she gets sick in all of 'em. And George, the only time he gets away is to Littlehampton wiv the swimming club.'

'I suppose you think that'll cheer me up,' observed Henny gloomily. 'But right now it doesn't. I'll just have to think of something.'

'Rob a bank.'

'Write a hit record.'

'Find some stolen jewellery and claim the reward.'

'Go out busking.'

'What's that?'

'You know—you stand in the street or the station and play the violin or the guitar, and people throw money in a hat.'

'But you can't play the violin. Or the guitar.'

'That *is* a problem,' said Henny. 'There always seems to be something between me and riches beyond the dreams of avarice, whatever that means.'

'Better wash me 'ands before I go in, or Sir'll be on at me again,' said Kim. 'I'll keep me eyes open, Henny. You never know what might turn up.'

Two days later she chased after Henny on the way to school.

'Hey! Wait for me! Look what I found!'

Panting, she caught up with her, waving a piece of newspaper in her face.

'Cor, it's far too 'ot to run! Look, I seen this last night an' I tore it out for you special.'

'Stop flapping it around, then! Let's have a look. What is it?'

'It's a competition. You know Dad gets piles of papers to use in the shop? Well, he got a whole lot yesterday, and I spotted this while I was wrapping up spinach for Mrs Staples. See? It's just what you need.'

' "Win a Great Last Chance Family Holiday!" ' read Henny slowly. ' "Here's *your* chance to win the holiday of a lifetime! Have you ever wished to spend a Happy Family Holiday doing what you want where you want, plus money to do it with? All you have to do ..." '

'It's a big travel company, see,' interrupted Kim. 'Me Dad explained it. They got 'olidays left no one's bought yet, so they're running this competition, and they're giving away three 'olidays—three *family* 'olidays—as prizes, and then they tell everyone what sends in about all the other 'olidays they 'aven't sold, so as to get them to buy them. But just imagine if you won a prize!'

'That'd be great! Just think—we could go to Spain ...'

'Or France ...'

'Or Italy even. Ooh, Kim, do you really think I *could* win? There's only three prizes.'

'It does say "Many consolation prizes too", but I

don't see why you shouldn't win. Besides, you ain't 'eard the best bit yet.'

They stopped to wait for a gap in the traffic.

'No, what?'

'We got at least a dozen of those papers, so you can cut out all the coupons. That way you'd 'ave at least twelve chances!'

'Cor, Kim, that'd be terrific! But don't you want a go?'

'No, 's all right. Me Mum says she did abroad when she was eighteen and she didn't reckon it much then, and anyway we're all booked up and she ain't going to change now. So you go right ahead.'

They heard the bell ringing, and started to run.

'Thanks, Kim! All right if I come round to the shop tonight?'

'Sure, I'll tell me Mum.'

It thundered during the day, and great fat single drops of rain left great fat round marks on the dusty windows like giant fingerprints. Then it rained faster and faster until there were puddles in the playground and the windows were washed clean.

When Henny walked home the air felt damp and fresh, and sparrows were sitting in small pools busily spraying water over themselves. She found herself singing as she banged on the door and waited for Michael to open it.

'Got your temper back then? I bought you an ice pop. It's in the fridge.'

'Hey, terrific!' She rushed past him. Jack was sitting in the kitchen doorway, humming as he licked a red ice lolly which had been sucked pale pink. 'Hi, Jack! Had a good day?'

Jack nodded, grinning cheerfully, and a trickle of pink slid down his fingers. Henny bopped him gently on the head as she passed by, and opened the fridge.

'Michael, I'm going round to Kim's for a bit—all right?'

Kim was sitting in the kitchen behind the shop with a cup of tea and a pile of papers on the table in front of her.

' 'ere they are then. I got to go and find some scissors. Me Mum said to cut the coupons out neatly, she wants the papers afterwards. I'll 'ave a look upstairs.'

Henny sat down and began turning the pages of the top paper. There seemed to be an awful lot of pages and an awful lot of words. She had to go through it twice before she spotted it, the 'Win a Great Last Chance Family Holiday Competition'.

She read right through to the small print at the end.

'...for full details of prizes, rules and conditions, write to bla bla bla. Closing date: all entries must be received by June 15. Successful competitors will be notified by July 10.'

Kim came clattering down the stairs.

'Got them!'

'Kim! What's the date today?'

'I'm not sure. I don't remember. I know! It was the 13th yesterday, because Mark said it was lucky it wasn't Friday. So today's the 14th.'

'That means the closing date's tomorrow!'

'We ain't got much time. Better get going.'

'When's the last post?'

'Don't know. I'll ask me Mum.'

Kim returned. 'Nine o'clock, she thinks. As long as you post it wiv a first-class stamp you'll be O.K. I got the cabbage-cutting knife from next door. It'll be quicker wiv two of us.'

Together they bent over the pile of papers, and for the next few minutes there was no sound but the rustle of paper, the snip of scissors, the thin cutting noise of Kim's knife.

'There!' said Henny, folding up the last paper. 'That's the lot!'

'How many does that make?'

'One, two, three ... eleven, twelve, thirteen. Fourteen counting the one you gave me this morning.'

'You jolly well ought to be able to win with all those entries!' There was a sudden shout from next door of 'Kim! Shop!'

'I better go. Mum's on 'er own this afternoon. The van's playing up so Dad took it to be seen to.'

'I'll be off home then. Thanks a lot!'

' 's all right. Coming, Mum! Best of luck, anyway.'

'Mum not back yet?'

'No. She rang to say she'd be late. What're you doing?'

Michael peered over Henny's shoulder as she sat down at the kitchen table and took the coupons out of her pocket.

'Winning us a holiday.'

'You've got a hope!'

'Yes, I have. Why shouldn't I?'

He glanced at the instructions.

'They're all the same, these competitions. It's just a gamble. I bet they get hundreds and *hundreds* of entries. It's just luck whether you pick the right numbers and arrange them how they choose.'

'You *are* cheerful, I must say! At least I've got fourteen chances. You just wait and see!'

He snorted, and went off back to his room, while Henny sat down to think.

What, in her judgement, were the seven factors which contributed most to making a family holiday happy? 'Choose from the nine listed below and arrange in the order of importance; for example, if you think "A sandy beach" is most important, put c) in Box 1.'

Henny read the list through.

'a) Special meals for children.

b) Baby-sitting services.

c) A sandy beach.
d) Good weather.
e) Evening entertainment for parents.
f) Close to shops.
g) Separate swimming pool for toddlers.
h) Near public transport.
i) Reasonable prices.'

She began to see what Michael meant.

For a start, which two should she leave out? 'Evening entertainments' didn't sound essential, but then parents might not agree. 'Close to shops' didn't sound exciting—who wanted to spend a holiday trailing round shops?—but then if there weren't any at all where would they be able to buy icecream and postcards?

'Hey, Jack,' she said, as he trotted into the kitchen and made for the biscuit tin, 'what would you rather have on holiday, a sandy beach or a safe swimming pool?'

He paused for a moment before opening the tin.

'Both,' he said simply.

'*You're* no help! Only *one* custard cream, there's hardly any left.'

She got up to remove the tin from him, and sat down again, nibbling thoughtfully at the pen.

Michael was right. She'd simply have to trust to luck. She went to get some paper, and settled down to working out suitable combinations, scattering the numbers around to create as much variety as possible. It took a surprisingly long time before she got fourteen sets which satisfied her. Then carefully she copied each one out on its coupon. Now she had to think about the final line.

'Complete in not more than ten words: "I would like to win a Great Last Chance Family Holiday because ..." '

She brooded.

'... Because we haven't enough money to pay for one.'

She wrote it down and looked at it.

It was true enough, but it didn't seem to have a prizewinning ring.

'... Because my big brother is going to scout camp and my little brother and I can't go away.'

That wouldn't do. It sounded whiney, and anyway it was too long.

She sighed.

Why wasn't Mum back? She'd be able to help. She looked at the clock. Poor Mum. She was *very* late tonight. And the night before she'd been late too. She'd looked so tired, and Henny herself hadn't exactly helped.

Suddenly the words flew into her mind.

'... Because my Mum works very hard for us all year.'

She counted the words. There was room for one more. She added 'so' to 'very', and sat back content.

Patiently she pulled the coupons back towards her and completed the line fourteen times. She had to write much smaller than usual to squeeze it all in, and her hand ached by the time she'd finished.

Still, at last it was done. She sat back and looked at her work. Surely one of them would win? She went to her room, and scrabbled around until she unearthed the writing-set Grandpa Cary had given her for Christmas. Luckily there were still two envelopes left. She picked the one with a horseshoe in the lefthand corner, put the coupons inside, and stuck down the flap.

'Michael!' She paused at the door to his room. 'Do you know where the stamps are?'

He was lying propped up on his bed by the open window, with exercise books and pieces of paper strewn around him. He paid no attention.

'Michael! I need a stamp!'

'Shove off, Henny. I'll have a look in a minute. I'm busy working.'

She came in the room.

'You're not!' she accused. 'You're reading *Asterix*, I can see it from here.'

'Never mind, I'm not moving until I've finished it, so you'll just have to wait.'

He raised the book higher, and placed it pointedly between him and Henny.

'Pig!' she said automatically, but there was plenty of time, and besides she suddenly realised that she was extremely hungry. It was ages since dinner, and what with rushing off to get the coupons, and then having to fill them in, she'd been too busy to eat anything but a couple of biscuits.

She propped the envelope on the shelf out of Jack's way, and set to work to make herself some sandwiches. She made two of salad cream and one of golden syrup, and sat down on the back doorstep to eat them. Jack, who had been sitting outside playing some complicated game with his cars and a couple of cardboard boxes, came and sat companionably beside her and ate half of them, so she had to get up and make some more.

It was great sitting there in the warm fresh air, even if there was nothing to look at but the brick wall dividing their house from Mr Marston's. Henny sat on comfortably, occasionally helping Jack by vrooming his cars towards him.

She had worked her way through several sandwiches, the last biscuits, and a mug of milk, and was halfway through an apple before she realised that Michael had still not appeared.

Muttering, she jumped to her feet.

Michael hadn't moved; only his book had changed.

'MICHAEL! WHAT ABOUT MY STAMP? I NEED A STAMP TO POST THE LETTER TO WIN US ALL A HOLIDAY AND I'VE GOT TO POST IT *TODAY*!'

'You're a pest, Henny!' But reluctantly he put down

his book, and swung his legs off the bed. 'I'll have a look in the front room. Mum's usually got some stamps there somewhere.'

He wandered off down the hall, and peered among the various pots and jugs and ornaments on the mantelpiece.

'I'm not sure ... Maybe she's run out ... Success! Here's one under its paw.' He lifted up the china cat covered with painted flowers, and handed Henny the stamp. 'You're in luck. It looks like the last one.'

Henny looked at it.

'But that's not first class, is it?'

'Doesn't matter. It'll get there just the same.'

'But Mike, it's got to get there *tomorrow* or it'll be too late! Are you *sure* there isn't another one?'

'Not as far as I can see. 'Tell you what, ring the upstairs bell and ask the Nicholsons.'

'I bet they're not there. Ever since it's been so hot, I haven't heard them come back till ever so late.'

Picking the envelope off the shelf, she ran outside and rang the bell, and waited, and rang again, and then rang and rang; but there was no answer.

What about Mr Marston?

She ran next door, and waited impatiently, banging the knocker and peering through the letter box, until at last she saw his slippered feet coming towards her.

'Hello, Henny! Come along in, love. I was sitting in the garden with Toffee. He loves this weather, and so do I. I remember, when I was a lad ...'

He led the way down the hall and through the kitchen and out into the back, still talking, while Henny danced with impatience.

Mr Marston's long skinny garden had a thin strip of grass and runner beans and tomatoes growing against the wall on the sunny side. Toffee lay sprawled on a patch of warm soil, very large and fluffy and ginger and content. He opened his eyes as Henny came near him, and then shut them again. Henny bent down to stroke him. Toffee purred, and sprawled, and stretched even flatter than before.

'What a happy cat, eh?' said Mr Marston approvingly.

'Mmm, he certainly looks it ... Mr Marston, what I wanted to ask you is, do you have any stamps?'

'I don't believe I do, pet. I'll 'ave a look though.' He tickled Toffee under the chin with his foot.

'Mr Marston, would you mind *very* much looking right away? You see, I've got to catch the last post.'

'The last post!' He sucked his breath in sharply. 'Oh, Henny, I think you've just about missed it.'

'I can't have! Mrs Macgregor said it went at nine. I don't know what time it is, but it isn't anywhere *near* as late as that! Why, that's after my bedtime, never mind Jack's!'

'I'm afraid she's made a mistake, love. It goes at seven, I know, because I write to me sister every week, never fail, and I always gets it in for the last post. I tell you what, I bet your Mrs Macgregor saw the notice on the letterbox that says last post 19 hours, and I wouldn't mind betting you she thought it said 9 o'clock. It's this 24-hour clock, see, fools a lot of folk.'

'Oh, no! What time is it?'

'Almost seven. Look, I'll give you some money, here you are love, you go round to the letterbox now, put it into the stamp machine, let's hope it's working, and maybe you'll just be in time. But you watch the road mind! We don't want no accidents now, do we?'

Henny thanked Mr Marston and tore off down the street, round the corner into the main road, past the baker's, the chemist's, the launderette and the pub. At the next turning she saw the letterbox, and next to the letterbox she saw the post office van. She started across the road. A car hooted, and she jumped back, heart beating. The car passed her. Then a motor bike. Then a van came down in the opposite direction, closely followed by a very slow building lorry laden with broken bricks and concrete. When it had passed she saw the post office van beginning to move.

She raced across the road, shouting and waving her envelope in the air, hoping against hope that the driver would see her in his mirror.

But the van drove away.

She reached the letterbox and leaned on it, panting.

In the little square panel over the mouth it said: 'Next post: No. 1.'

She felt tears gathering and starting to spill over her eyelids. She couldn't help it.

'What's up, lass? It can't be as bad as all that, nothing is. What's the matter, Henny? ... It *is* Henny, isn't it?'

Henny nodded, blinking her eyes to clear the tears away.

It was Mark's Dad.

He pushed a couple of envelopes into the box.

'What's the trouble? I heard you calling when I was crossing the road. Missed the post, did you? Well, it's not the end of the world, is it?'

Forcing back the tears, Henny explained about Kim and the holiday and the competition and the stamp and how after everything she'd arrived too late.

Mr Sinclair listened.

'Not to worry! All is not lost. Look—it says here there's a later collection from the district post office at 21 hours. That's nine o'clock. There's plenty of time to catch that.'

'But I don't even know where it is, and if I did ...'

'Hold on, hold on! *I'll* take it.'

'You'll take it?'

'Yes. It's no bother. I know where it is. I'll pop along in the van. Here, give it to me ... Oh, and you'll want another stamp, won't you? I've got some here in my wallet. Always have some handy for keeping in touch with my family. I've got brothers and sisters all over the place. That's all right, you hang on to your money. I don't know what sort of fix Mark got himself in when we moved here, but I do know that you helped him and one good turn deserves another. So don't you fret now, and the very best of luck. When will you hear if you've won?'

'July 15.'

'I'll keep my fingers crossed for you. Cheerio!'

Henny ran back home feeling positive she was going to win. It was lucky Kim's parents had got the papers, lucky Kim had seen the competition, lucky that she'd managed to finish it just in time, lucky to have Mr Sinclair turn up and make sure she caught the post.

Why shouldn't she be lucky once more?

Sometimes during the next few weeks she still felt sure she was going to win. At other times she was equally sure she wasn't.

The last week of waiting was the hardest.

On the night of July 14 she lay awake for what seemed like hours, and fell asleep at last to dreams of walking along a beach covered in deck chairs, every one sat in by a dozing holidaymaker, and following a deckchair man dressed like a bus conductor who kept churning out tickets.

In the morning she woke with a jolt, swung herself off her bunk and raced down the hall.

Three envelopes lay on the mat.

She stood there half afraid to pick them up.

The first one was a brown envelope with the sort of transparent window which usually meant a bill.

The second was a blue envelope addressed to her mother in what she recognised as Granny Lindsay's writing.

Very slowly, she turned over the last one.

It was from the library and addressed to Michael.

Michael came out of his room and stood yawning.

'Were you lucky? Did you win?'

Henny shook her head, not trusting herself to speak.

'Never mind, Hen. It was a jolly good try. Better luck next time.'

Mrs Cary came out from the front room with her dressing gown over her shoulders.

'Cheer up, Henny! It was super of you to try so hard. Come on now, breakfast. It's still early, we can have something special. What would you like?'

All the people she told at school—Kim and Arabella and Mark and Kevin and Dennis—were sympathetic too; but they forgot about it almost as soon as they'd asked, Henny thought. She felt gloomy all day, even though it was her almost-favourite pudding, apricot crumble and ice cream, and in the afternoon they went to the park to do some training for sports day.

She walked home slowly, feeling the difference from the day before. Today there was nothing to look forward to.

Michael started talking before she was even through the door.

'Hey, Henny, look! A letter came for you by second post!'

She grabbed it and tore open the top.

'Hurry up! Read it! What does it say?'

'Dear Competitor,' she started slowly, 'we are happy to tell you that you have won,' she said with mounting excitement, 'a prize in our recent Great Last Chance Family Holiday competition. We are enclosing herewith a voucher for' her voice fell, 'a bottle of champagne, which can be redeemed by anyone over 18 at ...' She stopped and looked up at Michael. 'A bottle of champagne! What good's that?'

'Well, it might not be a holiday,' Michael said

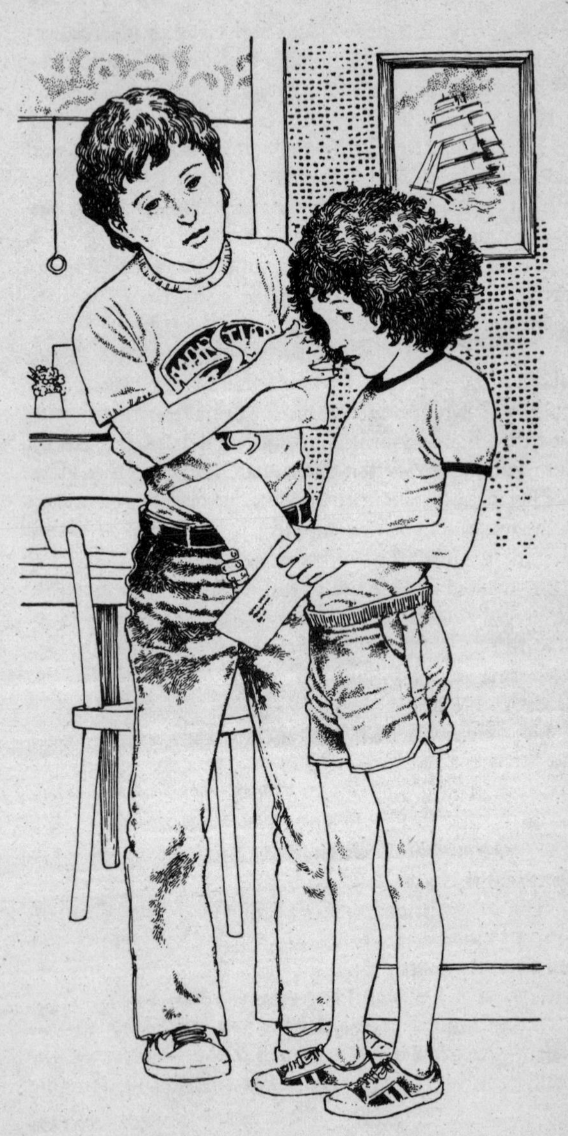

briskly, as he led the way down the hall, 'But I bet you Mum won't say "what good's that?" Congratulations, Henny! I've never met anyone who won anything in a competition before.'

And he was right, for Mrs Cary, as soon as she heard the news, said 'Hurray, Henny! How clever of you! I'll go round straight after supper to swop the voucher, and we can all have a sip.'

But she was still slicing onions when the door bell rang.

It was Mark and his father.

Henny asked them in and took them back to the kitchen.

'It's like this,' said Mr Sinclair, after the initial hellos were over. 'I asked Mark when I got back if Henny'd heard about her competition, and when Mark told me she hadn't been lucky after all I came round to make a suggestion. I got a letter from one of my sisters yesterday. They've got a farm in Derbyshire, and they've a little cottage they let out in the summer. She says they've just had a cancellation from the people who were going to take it at the beginning of August. She wondered if we'd like to come instead. Mark and me can't go then—I can't get away 'til later—and I wondered if you would be interested? It's a nice place, we went two years ago. I know you'd be comfortable. And it wouldn't cost anything. The people who couldn't come are paying through some insurance, and my sister wouldn't have time to let it properly even if she wanted to. So if you'd like to go ...?'

'I think we'd like that very much! Thank you, Mr Sinclair. Won't you stay and have a bite of supper, and tell us more about it?'

'I wouldn't want to put you out, Mrs Cary.'

'You won't at all. It'll be a pleasure. And tell you what,' she reached up and picked the voucher off the shelf, 'how about going round the corner and changing this for us? Henny *did* win something after all! A consolation prize. And a very good consolation too!'

There was a loud pop and the cork shot through Mr Sinclair's fingers and hit the ceiling.

'Mud in your eye!' said Jack suddenly.

'That's what telly does for you,' said Michael. 'It'll be the ruin of the younger generation.'

Mrs Cary carefully poured out six glasses. Two big ones for herself and Mr Sinclair, three small ones for Michael and Henny and Mark, and one tiny one for Jack.

'Here's to Henny!' Mrs Cary raised her glass in the air.

'To Henny!' echoed the others.

'Thank you,' said Henny. She took a cautious sip. The champagne fizzed and sparkled and tickled her nose. 'Sort of funny, but nice. I'm glad you like it. Still, I'm sorry I didn't win us a holiday.'

'But you did! Don't you see? If you hadn't done all those competition entries, then you wouldn't have met Mark's father when he went to post them, and he'd never have thought of us when he got his sister's letter yesterday. So you did get us a holiday after all. Didn't you?'

'I suppose I did,' said Henny slowly. 'In a sort of a way. Well, happy holiday everyone!'

The champagne swung and glittered in the raised glasses; and Toffee, sitting on the kitchen sill where he loved to come and sit, twitched his shoulders at the shouts of 'Happy holiday!' tucked his paws firmly under him, and settled back to sleep.

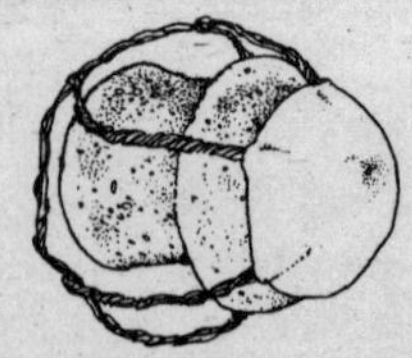